Woman on the Road

by Joy Harmon

This is a work of creative non-fiction, not a biography in the classic sense.. All of the events described herein really happened to me or to persons in my life. The time frame, the names, and some details have been changed. This is the way I remember the events, not necessarily the way they happened. Details describing events in the lives of others are included to clarify my relationship to them and the impact they had on my life. Some events happened before I knew them, in which case I pieced the events together to make them fit the story.

Editor: Nancie McKinnon coastaledit@gmail.com
Cover photo: Bruce Jenkins

Copyright © 2017 Joy Harmon
All rights reserved.
ISBN-13:978-1981663071
ISBN-10:198166307X

Create Space

FOREWORD

This story has no overriding message or moral. The idea is to show my life in little snapshots of people and events that shaped who I became. First and foremost, it is meant to be an entertaining read. If you take anything away from it, other than a few laughs and tears, perhaps it will be a closer look at your own life. We are shaped by family backgrounds, education, and careers, yes. Sometimes though, it is a small encounter, a serendipity, that flips our view of the world, creating a change in our direction and point of view. In the end, it's your book, the moment you open it and begin to read.

Enjoy!

INTRODUCTION

I originally thought this novel was going to be all about road trips, train travel, and flight. Maybe the only thing it really turned out to be is flight. It seems I am forever leaving or arriving somewhere. But the real story is about the people I meet along the way. My personal story is not complete, but a certain phase of my life is. Life is only partly about experiences and people. What it's really about is who you are and how all these experiences and people affect you and contribute to who you are.

I'm not offering up any key to who I am or solutions to your life. I'm just saying, "Take a look. This is what happened to me. These are the people, places, and events that stayed with me. This is what lead me to accept myself and my world. How is yours?"

ACKNOWLEDGMENT

Special thanks to Nancie McKinnon who generously gave her time, expertise, input, and support to this, my first novel. In addition, thanks to Steve Meyer, who along with writers' group members Allan and Judith, patiently listened to early chapter versions of this book, offering encouragement, and invaluable advise. Without them, I don't think I would ever have had the courage to publish this book.

CONTENTS

1 How I got there 1
2 Honolulu 5
3 L.A. 7
4 Topanga Hitchhiker 11
5 The Definition of Success 15
6 A Woman's Place 17
7 An Open Door 23
8 Fire 27
9 Scotland 29
10 Ladies Auxiliary Luncheon 35
11 Columbia River Gorge 41
12 Losing the Tether 47
13 The East Coast 51
14 Ken 57
14 Revenge 65
16 The Webster 69
17 A Circus Life 73
18 The Minnesota Nice and a Crisis 79
19 The Southwest Route 85
20 Vegas Show Girl 93
21 San Francisco 101
22 Wheels 107
23 The Man at the End of the Platform 109
24 Green Card 113
25 The Lady in the Chanel Suit 117
26 Strange Neighbors 119
27 Ex-cons 121
28 Snuff 127

29 Chance meeting 131
30 The San Francisco Hiker 133
31 The Bond Thief 135
32 Abe 137
33 Ocean Beach Mystery House 143
34 Scherenschnitte 145
35 Hotel El Rancho 149

PROLOGUE

TRAVELING IS IN MY BLOOD

Traveling began early. My mother and father were married during war time and it was easy for them for a while. My father was young, too young for the draft at first. But like all the other young men, he felt he should be doing his part. But he had another obligation; my mother was probably pregnant. It was never spoken of in our house and it didn't even occur to me until I was quite a bit older. I never asked about it and I never asked my older brother. He would have gotten angry and denied it in any case. I had looked up to him during my teen years and I didn't want to risk destroying my relationship with him. As for my mother, she would have slapped me, and a slap is not an answer. Perhaps it was none of my business anyway. By that time I was worrying about my own future and I put aside this question.

1 HOW I GOT THERE

I had made my way to Hawaii on vacation after working in retail for a year to save money. I was in love with it even before we landed. As we came in sight of Oahu and circled for the landing, I could see the mountains looking like furry green carpets. It was like a place in a fantasy. Everywhere you looked there were flowers and greenery. There were no large reptiles and no snakes. The island was serpent free and inspections of all incoming cargo kept a close watch in order to prevent any stowaway invaders into the islands of Hawaii. It truly was paradise to me.

I checked into the YWCA just off Waikiki. My brother was stationed at the base in Kaneohe on the other side of the island. There were no cell phones but I had left a message where I was staying. I entertained myself by walking on the beach in the morning and doing a little research on the job market in the afternoon. I hadn't told anyone that I planned on staying. The first thing was to get a job.

It was the off season and Waikiki was not too commercial, so it was relaxing to just walk around. Besides the beach, there was a free zoo further up Kalikaua Avenue, which was the main drag in Waikiki. There were a few upscale restaurants and hotels, but in those days, the beach wasn't lined with high rise hotels like Miami Beach. Even the Royal Hawaiian Hotel, the island's most famous hotel, was a row of low pink bungalows. The main entertainment was in the traditional market and cultural center. It would have free entertainment in the evenings. And there were an array of small shops and inexpensive eateries with outside tables, where you could sit as long as you liked with just a drink. Of course, there were the beverages in coconut shells, but my favorite treat was the a frozen chocolate dipped banana.

I had been hanging out there the first evening and when I got back, the custodian told me I'd had visitors. He described them as two military men, even though they weren't in uniform, he recognized the posture and the walk. I walked back up the street to see if I could find them. It had to be my brother and a friend. It didn't take long. They were sitting on the wall in front of the cultural center watching people go by and hoping to see me. My brother wasn't happy when I told him the custodian had known they were in the military. Marine training sticks. He ended up working at Cape Canaveral after his stint in the Marines. I remember the same expression on his face years later, when I asked how he liked working at the Cape.

It didn't take long for me to make my own friends and I got by sleeping on the beach or hanging out with friends until I found a job.

I ended up in a little apartment near Everybody's Market in Honolulu with two rooms screened in and no glass. I hadn't known that it was common to have only screens in the windows in tropical climates before then. Even the big homes near Diamond Head were built this way. They had deep overhanging eaves which kept out the rain, and shutters that could be closed during typhoons. It did keep the houses cooler. Once you start putting in glass, there's always the heat generated by sunlight passing through glass, even with the windows open.

The Pumehana Street apartment was a hideout and only a few people knew where I lived. My parents started inquiring when I wasn't back in two weeks and my brother was looking, too. I didn't even communicate with my friends back home. I loved them, but I knew sooner or later someone would feel morally obligated to tell what they knew. My escape had been years in the planning, and I didn't want to be one of those teenagers that got picked up and sent back home after a few weeks. My parents weren't the kind to forgive you easily. I definitely didn't want to find out how they would react when they got me back. They'd probably lock me in the house for months. I would be eighteen in six months. I just had to make it until then.

That little apartment complex is probably long gone now, but I still remember it was on Pumehana Street just across the street from Everybody's Market. It was a set of six little one bedroom apartments, screened in and divided by tongue and groove panels. Most of the apartments faced the parking lot, but mine had a side entrance facing

Pumehana Street. If you came in from Pumehana Street, the address and apartment number were clearly marked and it looked like it should be the front door. One afternoon, I was just showering after getting home from my shift at the supermarket and I heard a knock at the door. I called out and asked who it was. I was leaning around the bathroom doorway, trying to see the front door, which was off the kitchen. It was the mailman and he had a package.

"I can't come to the door. I'm in the shower."

I heard a voice say, "OK, I'll just leave it right here."

When I got out of the shower and went into the bedroom to get dressed, the package was on the bed, which was right by the door. He'd been at the back door and he'd had a full view!

It wasn't easy for a houli, an outsider, to find work in Hawaii. Lots of young people came in summer with plans for a working vacation. So, most places wouldn't hire anyone who had lived in Hawaii for less than a year. There were some exceptions. Factories didn't pick and choose. Anyone could do that work and they were always looking to replace people who didn't show up. I worked in the pineapple factory for a few weeks until I could find something else. The work was ok, but it was obvious I wasn't going to fit in with my co-workers. The usual way they got acquainted in the cafeteria was to ask, "Are you married? You got kids?" The first question I avoided and the second became irrelevant.

My next job was in a grocery store where I got to watch a lot of interesting people shop. There were the elderly little Chinese women who stacked everything neatly in their cart and had the balance calculated by the time they reached the check out. If I was one penny off she'd know it. Then there were the big island mamas who swaggered down the aisles and just tossed things into the cart. Sometimes it seemed as it they just swatted the boxes of cereal off the shelf and yet they landed in the cart.

At break time, I would sit and listen to the local employees gossip in pidgin English. I picked up the idea pretty quickly. They just used the essential words, no changing verb tenses or elaborate definitives. After a while I realized that it wasn't just that it was a new way of speaking English.

Sometimes I could tell by their responses that they didn't understand each other. But the conversation never lagged. No one explained or clarified anything, they just carried on. I guess it would have been impolite to draw attention to the fact that your companion had misunderstood.

In my travels, I have often observed how English is adapted for use as the linqua franca among people who don't have a common native language. Often times, they will adapt words and expressions to their liking and use their native pronunciation for words they don't know. This stylized English is so often used that they are used to it and mostly understand each other regardless of what country they are from, even when I do not. If they get stuck on a word, there will be long discussions about a particular word or phrase. Slang will throw them off if they are not familiar with American style English and culture. One afternoon we spent about five minutes discussing the expression "edgy" One thought it meant fat and another something pointy. They laughed at the idea of a fat person with sharp pointy fat instead of soft rolls of fat.

Back in the grocery store, I got along best with the bag boys. They were closer to my age and could clue me into what was happening in Hawaii. I was never very good at checkout. I stayed there until I got fired for being too slow. It was time to move back to the mainland where jobs were easier to find and I could get lost in a bigger population. But I will always miss the mild climate and those soft green fur covered hills that look.

2 HONOLULU

Most of my adventures were fun, rather than embarrassing. There was a small band of hippies who traveled around the island in a van, stopping at will to play their drums and dance. One time I came upon them in the forest and spent a happy afternoon dancing among the trees in a beautiful Hawaiian forest. Another time a group of local bands got together and put on a free concert in the Punch Bowl. The Punch Bowl is a giant crater left from an extinct volcano which includes a national cemetery. I'm not exactly sure how they got electricity in there, but it was a great concert. The punch bowl shape made it perfect for viewing the concert. You could just lie back on the grass and look down into the center of the crater where the stage was set up.

Hawaii also turned out to be the location of my very first rock concert. It could have been anything, but it was my good luck that it turned out to be Jimi Hendrix. He had given a concert the night before and had not been satisfied with the sound. So, at the end of the concert, he had announced that he would give a free concert the following night for anyone who had a ticket from that night's concert. A friend had heard it on the radio, so we went down to the parking lot of the Hula Bowl, which was the big outdoor venue in Waikiki, and searched the parking lot for discarded tickets. It didn't take long. There were always people who left early or just couldn't make it back the next night. They always just tossed the tickets on the ground. In this case, littering was a very good thing. We found enough tickets for ourselves and all our friends.

The week before the concert, Kilauea Volcano on Hawaii had been erupting. You could see where the orange sky faded into a purple glow from Mount Tam. The entire sky was lit up in a purplish glow. Hendrix had been visiting a retreat on Maui at the time it started and the sky was putting on its display during the concert. So, when he played Purple Haze that night, it had a special significance. I don't know when that song was actually written, but I'll always remember it as the night I saw the purple sky from Kilauea. Some say it's about a drug trip; some say it's about the volcano. I think it's more likely both.

Hendrix was an interesting performer to watch. He played well and wasn't thinking about the time. Like some other performances I would later see, there were some long riffs where he got lost in the music. He'd do one of these long riffs, then turn it over to the band for a few minutes while he wandered off behind the big speakers set up on either side upstage. I was sitting just off to the side and I could see the roadie behind one of the speakers holding his joint for him. He'd go back there for a few minutes while the band carried on, take a toke and go back out and start up again. It was a crazy time. The Vietnam War was causing major protests on the mainland. The Black Panthers were at their strongest in Philly, Oakland, and L.A. They were literally at war with the police. There had been riots on college campuses around the country, as well. But I wasn't thinking about all that. I was thinking about Jimi Hendrix and a real purple haze!

Jimi's response to the turmoil in the streets back in the mainland was his personal arrangement of The Star Spangled Banner. It was loud; it was irreverent, it was mean; and it was totally recognizable in all its electric power. He played the audience out with that song and we all cheered the music and booed the cops. When I think back on it now, it was kind of mean. The Hawaii cops were not aggressive. Their biggest task was keeping the flow of drugs to a minimum and they did it with a light hand. Police harassment in Honolulu amounted to being asked for your I.D. in front of your friends. You'd have to be pretty careless to get arrested. Soldiers would occasionally get into fights in bars, but they would just arrest them and call the MPs to take them back to their respective bases.

I could have stayed there forever. But I made a choice that ended up in LA. I can't say I regret that, it lead to everything else that's happened in my life. But I've always wondered if I wouldn't have been more content if I'd stayed in Hawaii. I probably would have ended up on Maui or Kauai going barefoot and working in a small shop

3 L.A.

LA was another new experience. I'd been used to hitchhiking around Oahu, but I learned quickly, this was not the thing in LA. In fact, walking wasn't the thing. For the first six months, I didn't have a car. They do have sidewalks there, but you can't go two blocks without some guy offering you a lift.

I borrowed a bicycle and rode to the fabric store, where I worked as a sales girl for a couple of months. Eventually, someone noticed me going by at about the same time every day and started following me. I knew all the back streets, so I zigzagged in and out until I got to the main street, ducked into the back through the parking lot, and hid inside the atrium under the staircase until the first manager got there and opened the doors. I got a car the next day.

So, I had to learn how to stay safe in Los Angeles, it was just training for San Francisco. Meanwhile, the City of Angels was a lot of fun for a few years. There was Dodger Stadium and my first time seeing a major league baseball game, hikes in the mountains, the zoo in Griffith Park, jazz concerts, and first run movies.

I was young and it was a time in my life that I could never live again. Weird things happen at night in Los Angeles. You don't have to party, you just have to go outside and wander around and you'll see something crazy. It was even a kick to go to the all night grocery store after midnight. There were no lines and if there was a cart blocking the aisle it was just some crazy or stoned person who'd wandered off and forgotten why they came to the store in the first place. You'd see them, going up and down the aisles lost. They'd finally find the section they were looking for, then just stand there and stare for about ten minutes. You'd finish your shopping, go to the check out, look down the aisle and they'd still be standing there. Eventually they'd come down enough to finish their shopping and come to the check out with a cart full of chips, soft drinks, cookies, and maybe a frozen pizza. Not that much different from a regular teenager diet.

High school students still cruised Van Nuys Boulevard, but I was an outsider now, to old for high school but not quite ready for adult life. My interests lay elsewhere. My friends and I would often cruise to the top of Topanga Canyon for the view of the lights in the long wide valley that is San Fernando Valley, just over the hills from Hollywood. The lights stopped at the mountain boundaries. In between, Van Nuys Boulevard ran all the way to Sherman Oaks on the south end and to Sylmar in the north, almost twenty miles of wide well lit streets. No wonder it was the cruise street.

But my friends and I had other destinations in mind. Sometimes we'd continue on through the canyon and go to the beach just north of Malibu. Just at the place where you have a sand dune on one side of the highway and the beach on the other, there's a beach that has phosphorescent sand at night. We liked to go there to kick up the sand and chase each other around. That was if the Malibu police didn't stop to harass you. The houses on the north end of Malibu were very upscale and the residents next to the beach considered it their own, even though it was technically a public beach. Night visitors weren't welcome.

One night, as we were crossing the highway to our car parked on the opposite side next to a sand dune, we saw them coming. It was winter, not too cold. But I had on a light coat with Dalmatian spots on it. The guys were in their usual jeans and dark jackets. When we saw the cops coming we started running, then crawling up the sand dune. There was a dip near the top where you could hide and both of the guys had just jumped into it. They weren't worried about me because I was just a few feet behind them. Just then the cops turned on the spotlight.

"Get down and don't move!" they whispered.

I went spread eagle in the sand and we could hear them calling us.

"Come on down. We know you're up there."

The light was flashing back and forth. After a few minutes they left. They weren't interested enough to climb up after us. As soon as they were out of sight, we ran, slid, and tumbled down the hillside to the car. Once in the car and heading the opposite direction, both guys started laughing. They had shined the spotlight directly on my back and didn't see me. The Dalmatian spots on the white coat just looked like spots in the sand!

4 TOPANGA HITCHHIKER

Topanga Canyon Boulevard cuts through Topanga State Park in the mountains before it descends to the beach at Malibu on the west side. Mostly you see a lot of trees, but you don't see any animals, except for the occasional vulture or hawk circling overhead. But if it's just before sunset of a quiet evening when there aren't any other cars around, you may see something crossing the road that reminds you that this small portion of a mainly urban area is still wild. Usually it will be a skunk or a raccoon. One evening just before sunset, I saw a bobcat up close. I'd only seen them in pictures. I've never seen one in a zoo or even out hiking up north in Sequoia or Yosemite. But it was unmistakable! It was crossing the road and as it turned to look straight towards me, I could see the distinctive slightly flattened face with the wings of whiskers coming out at the cheeks of that cat like head, a body too big to be a domestic cat, yet too small for a mountain lion. No other member of the North American big cat family is built like that.

Topanga Canyon is more a forest preserve than a developed park. There are no groomed trails. Hiking here is rough at best in the daytime and dangerous at night. But there was one place you could stop at night for a fine view within an easy walk. It was an abandoned ranger lookout station just at the top of the last ridge. It's a steep climb up, about fifty feet in the air to the little hut on the top, but worth it. You could see why it was there. There was a clear view down the canyon to Malibu and the coastline in either direction on the west with the whole San Fernando Valley visible to the east. It was the perfect place for a fire watch. Any smoke would be visible for miles. It was also a perfect place to watch fireworks on the Fourth of July. We got there just at dusk. The sun was down but it was still easy to see the steps. We found a good spot on the surrounding porch and sat dangling our legs over the edge. When the fireworks started, we could see the display on the beach on one side and all the different fireworks displays in the suburbs across the San Fernando Valley at the same time. Even some of the fireworks from northwest side of LA, which included Hollywood, Beverly Hills, and Century City could be seen above the hills looking south over Laurel Canyon.

As the night passed, a few other people who knew about this place showed up. After a while there were cars visible from the road and people who hadn't known it was there started showing up. It wasn't crowded but we had enough people for a good party, maybe twenty or so. Everybody seemed to be having a pretty good time. We were high up in the air with only the porch rail between us and a long drop. Nobody was getting rowdy. Everyone was just sitting or standing watching the fireworks and occasionally cheering.

Of course, the dozen or so cars parked on the forestry road and along the main road eventually attracted attention and the rangers showed up. Rangers are a pleasant bunch and there were no reprimands or threats like there might have been from L.A. city or county cops. They just politely asked us to come down and informed us that there was a danger because the tower wasn't meant to hold all that extra weight. Everyone came down quietly. The fireworks were about over anyway. We all headed home, with a good memory of that particular Fourth of July celebration. It was a whole lot better than getting drunk at someone's backyard barbeque. No insult intended, I've been to some pretty fine barbeques, but they didn't have a lookout tower.

On many of our trips up Topanga Canyon, our friend Jim would drive us in his 1938 Dodge Touring Car with the suicide doors. This is now a much sought after classic car. But back then it was shunned by the Van Nuys Boulevard cruisers, as an out of date grandpa car. It was the kind of car treasured by their grandparents, but not cool if you were into cruising. The coolest cars on the road had custom paint jobs and hydraulic suspension that allowed them to ride low to the ground. The look was long and lean. The feel was "slow and low." If you aren't familiar with this American cultural phenomenon, check out a film from the late 1970s called *Boulevard Nights*.

It's enough to know that there were always some car enthusiasts that understood that certain cars were classics or destined to be classics. But there were few enough of these classic collectors in those days and you could still get a nice older car for a song. If you had a good eye for quality, you could end up enjoying that car for years.

I don't know how long Jim kept that car, but it was special. Not only was it a special car that was reliable and easy to fix when it did have problems, but it was truly designed for touring. There was plenty of legroom in the front and back seats and those suicide doors opened forward, so getting in and out of the back was easy. Long car trips in the 1930s were a luxury, but there were no super highways. So all the comforts of travel had to be accounted for. The trunk was large and roomy, designed to carry trunks rather than suitcases. You would be driving through changing weather and on roads that were mainly paved, but not always. One website, (Mother Nature Network) estimates it took five days by train to travel coast to coast in 1930. With nearly 3,000 miles to travel on today's highways, it would be about 3 days driving non-stop, which is not practical. Top speed in 1930 was 50 miles per hour. It is likely that it would have taken more than a week to make the same trip, with rest stops, overnight stops and all the junctions that had to be maneuvered. So, this car had a very comfortable backseat, much like a sofa. You could really relax and enjoy the ride.

We were enjoying it one night on another Topanga run, when we saw a car broken down by the side of the rode in the canyon. The driver hailed us and asked if we could take him to his house to get some tools. It was here in the canyon and he promised to give us a non-monetary reward in the bargain. There was no hesitation on Jim's part. He'd stopped; he was a person who was always willing to help. He wasn't looking for payback. The offer of a little something extra along the way was just icing on the cake.

We went a couple of miles down a dirt road before we saw a nice little cabin up against a hillside. He invited us in and we all made ourselves comfortable in the front room. He packed up the tools he needed and rolled a couple, one for now and one for the road. He said he was a studio musician. It paid well and he got to work with a lot of big name recording artists. He lit up a number and there was some discussion among the guys about the quality. It was a kind of male rutting on a social level, only slightly competitive, but sizing each other up.

The stranger just smiled and said, " I only deal in psychedelic drugs," which seemed a little odd, since he was busy rolling that third doobie.

He pocketed the second one for later and let us pass the first one around as he began to play on an exquisite Martin guitar. It's hard to describe a musician's playing. To say, it's good, superior, or even fantastic, means nothing. What was evident right away was that we were watching an expert. It was just one guitar and it was mesmerizing. I am confident of my opinion, as I had plenty of time to take it in. The smoke came around slowly and I was the last to get a taste.

He didn't talk much, he just moved smoothly from one song to another. At one point, he paused and said, "Here's an unpublished Bob Dylan song." I have no idea if it ever became published or if this was all just talk. What I do know is that by that time I was sure this was no ordinary night. Things were looking all pleasant and sparkly.

We made our way slowly up the dirt road and back out onto Topanga Canyon Road to where his car was parked and dropped off our host. Jim asked if he needed us to wait around.

"No, but thanks for the lift."

"Thanks for the music," Jim responded and drove off.

We didn't stop to admire the view on the way back down to the valley. It was about three a.m. on Sunday morning by that time. And we would be wanting to sleep before we had to go back to work on Monday. As we reached the downhill side of the route, the road began winding along the cliff side of the hills. When it's steep like that and you are looking out a car window at a view that is far below you, it can feel like flying. In this case, it was more than that. The lines on the road seemed to be flying away, too.

We never saw the musician again. But he is a pleasant memory. Getting high, whether it is on alcohol, drugs, or some other means can be risky business. It's not always pleasant. But there are a few times when it is pure bliss. This was one of those.

5 THE DEFINITION OF SUCCESS

I chose Los Angeles as my next home and was able to stay with a friend of a friend in the San Fernando Valley. That was when I met Betty, the woman who taught me there was a different way to live.

She and her teenage son lived in a three bedroom house where she used the third bedroom as a studio. Betty was a weaver. There was a big floor loom in the studio and baskets of yarn all around the house. I had a small cot on one corner of the weaving studio.

Her son went to a small private school where students chose their own learning and teachers helped them. Nobody called them alternative schools back then. They had to learn about each subject, but how they learned was up to them. It must have worked well. He ended up with a full scholarship to Cal Poly and eventually became an engineer at JPL. Her older son was on his own but he would stop by occasionally and give me a ride home from work on his motorcycle.

Betty was busy preparing for The Renaissance Pleasure Fair, which had begun in 1963. By this time it had become an annual tradition with attendees coming from all over Southern California. As a weaver, Betty easily qualified as a vendor and was preparing card weaving kits for the crafty minded visitors at the fair. At that time, she was working exclusively as a weaver. In addition to working craft fairs, she did commission work for private collectors, interior designers, and the occasional set designer. She was a natural dyer and was featured in one of the current nature magazines for her experience and knowledge of natural dying techniques. She later moved to the Hollywood area and managed a fiber store that catered to weavers, spinners, and dyers. Knitters at that time still had Super Yarn Mart and most didn't give a thought to hand spun or hand dyed yarns. These could usually only be acquired from someone you knew who was a spinner or dyer. But mostly, weavers were the ones who really appreciated the hand dye process.

Betty was ahead of her time. She knew the value of making things was in the creation. In a world where everything was manufactured, she knew there was a difference in quality that could not be duplicated in mass production. It was an art form.

For me, it all started in my teens and carried on throughout my life. But Betty was the only person I knew who understood my devotion to making things in my teens and twenties when textile and fiber arts were not de rigueur. Making was about quality of life, not just keeping a homely art alive. When I visited her, we'd have tea and homemade cake or cookies while we discussed poetry, literature, and art. We lived in a world where life meant appreciating the beauty around you, whether it be your garden, a forest in the mountains, the latest innovations in art and music, or the art you created in your everyday life. The echoes of the Arts and Crafts Movement of the early 1900s were a part of this small counter culture. Although this time around, you didn't have to be rich to live the dream. We made things not because we had to, but because we celebrated life by creating beauty in our homes and personal lives.

Betty was my success story. I didn't want to be rich or famous. To me, success was finding a way to make a living doing what you loved. Betty did that. Even when she retired she continued to create. She sold the loom after she moved to Oregon, but kept the stash of hand dyed yarn. That Christmas she made a Kaffe Fassette designed cardigan for me from these bits and pieces of hand dyed yarn. It was like a history of her work in dying and weaving. Betty died the following summer and I cherished that sweater. I wore it until the seams fell apart and I regret giving it up. Now that I know more about knitting, I realize I could have salvaged the seams and gone on wearing it for another ten years.

6 A WOMAN'S PLACE

There was a big revival of quilting during my time in LA. Maybe it was the back to nature movement started by the hippies in the previous decade, or maybe people were just tired of polyester clothes, plastic furniture, and imitation wood. The quilting grew along with other hand crafts, but kept growing when other crafts lost their charm. It went from the bedroom to the wardrobe and back again. Shops were opening around the city that catered exclusively to quilters, quilting guilds sprang up, and the first national quilt shows appeared.

It was my interest in quilting and a desire to attend one of the first of these big shows that brought me together with many amazing women, one of whom had a major impact on my life. As my interest and ability in quilting grew, I began to visit the quilt shops. In one shop, a wonderful shop owner gave me an impromptu lesson on how to make a scrap quilt look unified through the use of color. She was a great teacher. She would talk a bit and then she would have me look at a quilt and talk about what I saw. She was leading me to my own conclusion; not by telling me, but letting me gradually come to see it for myself. That shop, like a lot of boutique shops, was in an upscale neighborhood where the customers had more expendable income. I was just a young woman and I am sure she knew I wasn't going to be a regular customer. Looking back on that experience, I appreciate it even more. She loved her work and was nice enough to take some time with me, without regard for making a sale. It was encouraging and, who knows, maybe it helped me stay interested in something that was to bring pleasure to my life for many years to come.

I kept exploring other quilt shops all around the San Fernando Valley, L.A. Proper, and all the way out to Santa Monica. There, in Santa Monica, I found a small quilt and craft shop called Crazy Ladies and Friends. It was owned by three friends, who each had a part of it. One of them, Mary Ellen, had the quilting. Mary Ellen was a dynamo of a woman! Small, energetic, and in love with life. She was one of the first shop owners to offer classes in her shop. I signed up for a class, just to see what I'd missed teaching myself.

It was a month long course covering all the basics of making a quilt, as well as history and source information about traditional designs. There was homework every week. She was no slouch, her students came away with a thorough knowledge of their craft. They wouldn't have a finished quilt, but they would have a start and an understanding of the commitment it would take to finish a long term project like this.

Mary Ellen's book, *It's OK If You Sit On My Quilt*, came soon after. It was so named, because of the guiding principle that a quilt was made to be loved and used. There should be no hesitation in piecing by machine; if done properly it looks just as nice as hand piecing and is much faster to complete. She emphasized that hand work was time consuming and took special skill. It should be saved for the places where it could be shown off.

It was through Mary Ellen that I attended my first quilter's meetup. Just like in days of old, ladies were getting together to help with hand quilting and socialize. It was amazing, just how similar these events were. They were always focused around quilting, good food, and good conversation.

In this case, many of the ladies brought completed projects, which were laid out in the living room. It was another cooperative learning experience for me. Because it was so casual, it was easy to talk to the maker of each quilt and hear its story. All quilts have stories. There is the historic background; what traditional design might have inspired the quilt? The personal background; who was it for or what experience inspired the quilt? And then, there was talk about the experience of making the quilt, as well. This often involved more stories about what happened in the quilter's life during the making of the quilt. Quilts take a long time, so a lot of stories and memories are stitched into those quilts.

After drinking tea and talking, we settled down to the host's quilt frame and I got a lesson in hand quilting.

"See how you rock the needle back and forth to make small stitches."

"See how a special thimble protects you from blisters and calluses from thousands of tiny stitches."

There was more talk round the quilt frame, as each person caught up with the others on how their lives were going. Who was sick and who was well? Who had a new baby? What was new in general? They weren't just concerned with domestic things. Many of them were involved in charity work or had other activities like running in local 10K races.

Mary Ellen summed it up beautifully.

"Look around this room. Every one of us is different. We have women whose ages range from their twenties to their seventies. We come from all different backgrounds and lives. Where else could you bring such a diverse group of women together, who all enjoy each other's company and care about each other, no matter their differences?"

Indeed! Quilting would bring me together with other caring women before that part of my life was over. But there was another similarity to olden times that was not so cheerful. As I found out when I signed up for a group trip to a quilt show in Northern California.

The first major show on the west coast was happening in Santa Rosa the following spring. Mary Ellen put an announcement on the board in the shop as soon as the news came out. She announced it in her classes and organized a group trip. With a small group, we could arrange a private plane to fly us there for less than the cost of a commercial flight and we would get a discount on rooms at a nice hotel. The list started filling up and it looked like the trip was a go. I was excited to see the work of quilt artists from all over the country. Many of them had new quilt books which had recently been published by major craft publishers. Craft books had a new face. They were colorful and fully illustrated and designed. They were breathing new life into a craft that had been mainly traditional for generations.

But about a month before the show, people started dropping out. First we lost the private flight, but adjusted our plans to include a commercial flight instead. Then we lost our discounted rooms. Finally, a couple of weeks before the show, there were just two people left, Mary Ellen and myself.

We weren't going to miss it. We flew to San Francisco and rented a car for the short drive north to Santa Rosa. We had to downgrade our ~~mmodation to an affordable but nice motel near the fairgrounds. I ~d a bit. It gave me a chance to get to know Mary Ellen better. to be going to this show with someone who was so

If you wa~~ ~~ ~~~ most out of a big show, whether it is at an art museum, a conven~ or like this one, at a fair ground, here's a method that works well.

This show took up three exhibition halls. The problem is you will get visual overload if you try to take it all in at once. That's why museums have coffee shops. It gives viewers a rest.\

On the first day, we did a walk around to get the lay of the land in the morning, during this round, we did an overview of the show. I marked off my program with the quilts I wanted to get a better look at on the following day. We went to lunch, then spent the afternoon in the vendors' hall. Even that was a show in itself. We had a nice dinner with a local wine that evening. Santa Rosa is just on the edge of the Sonoma County wine country. So, there was a nice selection at reasonable prices. We went happily off to bed, looking forward to our next day at the show.

The second day was taking a close look and getting pictures. I had a new camera and I took some good pictures of my favorites. It was an Olympus OM1 35mm camera and I had plenty of extra film in my bag. I didn't want to run out of film before I got all my favorites on a roll. It would be more than a decade before digital cameras were available for general use by the public and another ten years before the quality even came close to a SLR 35mm camera. Even today, I miss that camera.

We took the whole day going around the two quilt exhibition halls on the second day. Mary Ellen's extensive historical research for her book made her the an excellent guide. She knew the names of all the traditional patterns and could point out how the same pattern looked entirely different when used in an original way. There's a reason those traditional patterns are still with us today. They are the ones that have been presented in endless ways over the years and still look good with each new permutation. Each generation, right up to the modern quilter adds his or her own special details to create her own interpretation of a classic pattern.

But it wasn't all traditional colonial and pioneer quilts. The second hall had applique and free form quilts. There the traditional wedding applique quilts; Hawaiian quilts; and Mola designs, believed to have originated in Panama. What amazed me was how many of the quilters had used applique, embroidery, and quilting like a painter uses canvas. Some were breathtakingly beautiful, some were pictorial stories, some made political and social statements, and some made me laugh out loud. I'll always remember the quilt made entirely of bras! It wasn't pretty, but it certainly made a statement!

I learned more about quilting, quilt history, and women's history on that trip than I could have in a semester of women's history studies. I would continue to quilt for another ten years and meet many more amazing women along the way.

But I also learned a lesson about feminism through that experience. We had come a long way. Most of the women I knew under forty worked outside the home. They saw themselves as independent and in many ways they were. But the gradual dropping out of a weekend trip emphasized how many women still felt they had to have permission to do what they wanted to do. When I asked Mary Ellen why so many had dropped out, she said some had dropped out because of conflicts or extenuating circumstances, "but mostly, it was husbands. They didn't like the idea of their wives going off on their own with a group of other women."

That was 1977 and a lot has changed. Thankfully, one of those things is that women no longer feel they have to have permission. I also think they value the company of other women more than they did in the past. Family is still most important and always will be, but women have begun to see that the friendship of women is important. Guys have known this all along. They've always had their bonding groups, whether it was sports, college buddies, or professional organizations, they knew the value of companionship with other women. Women are learning.

7 AN OPEN DOOR

I met Lilith long before the road trips started. Back then a road trip meant a trip to the desert to watch the sunrise on New Year's Day or trip to the beach during a storm. I had a normal job and I thought I had a normal life. She knew differently.

I had a creative spirit that was locked in. I didn't see myself as being good at anything. I had given up music because I wasn't as good as the people around me. I gave up art because I knew I didn't have what it takes to be an artist. My plans didn't include suffering in poverty for years and never being recognized, which is the life of most artists. But that creative spark was still there. It came out in making bread, in sewing without following the directions, and keeping a secret diary.

Lilith knew. She saw something in me. She brought me into her fold and let me be the person I was meant to be. When I was with her, it was ok to be happy or sad, to feel joy and pain; I knew she would still be my friend.

She was a unique person in her own right. Her home was a sanctuary. The door was never locked. There was always a fire in the fireplace, except in the very hottest days of summer, and a tea kettle was always on within minutes of my arrival. She was a pagan, a mother, a quilter, and a crone. She had four beautiful children who were always in and out of the house. Even as they grew up and moved away, it was still home.

When I first met her, she read my cards. She didn't tell my fortune. She let me select the cards, placed each one in formation and described the symbolism of the card. Then she would ask me what that meant to me. This, she explained was divining.

"We don't tell fortunes, we don't promise love or predict death. The cards are a tool. They help to bring our thoughts inwardly when we have become too entangled in the physical world with all its distractions and problems. They help us focus."

We would drink tea, light candles, and lie by the fire; thinking and being. We let time stop for a few hours. In the early morning hours, I would find her at her quilt frame finishing a quilt with beautiful hand stitching which no machine can duplicate. There were quilts on all the beds; extra quilts in closets; and two trunks filled with quilts, one for each daughter. Each one would have a trunk with twelve quilts to take with her when she married or when she permanently left the nest on her own.

There had been a third daughter, but she had died at the age of five. There had been a fire in the house a couple of years before I met Lilith. Some of the story I learned from her and parts of it I learned from her another family member, and a close friend. I gradually put the pieces together.

Lilith and Eva, her eldest daughter, had been in the kitchen early in the morning before the rest of the house was up. Dora, the youngest, was playing in the living room. The bedrooms had been on the second story and they could hear one of the boys shouting at Sabine. Sabine was the very active third child and the boys would often get annoyed with her. So, they didn't think much about it at first. Then Eva noticed that smoke was coming out of the heating vent. Within moments, they smelled smoke and saw smoke coming from upstairs. The boys came running down stairs choking. They said they couldn't wake Sabine and they had tried and failed to reach her. Lilith tried to get to her but was overcome by smoke. Her oldest son had recovered by that time and tried again, but was unsuccessful. By that time the fire department was there. They told everyone to get out of the house and went upstairs for Sabine, but it was too late. She had died of smoke inhalation in her sleep.

They wouldn't let Lilith see the body. A close friend identified the body. She told me,

"I'll always remember the bedclothes were intact, but smoke blackened. When they lifted her up and carried her away, there was this little white shape where her body had been."

They buried her in the small town cemetery on a hill just up the road from their house. Her father, Ernie, had chosen the spot and had a tombstone with hearts and a little deer on it for her. He thought she would like that. He would go up there once a week to water the flowers they'd planted for her and to sit peacefully for a while.

Dora was a year older than Sabine. They'd wanted to have Sabine because the three other siblings were much older and they didn't want her to grow up alone. But now, despite their plan, Dora was growing up alone.

Dora was a charming little girl with long cocoa brown curls and big deep brown eyes. She loved everyone and wouldn't hesitate to come and sit in your lap and smile while you were chatting with the grownups. She was cheerful but quiet. I would sometimes have her to my house overnight. We'd have fun drawing or coloring, walking around the little town where I lived, and eating broccoli for dinner. Most kids don't seem to like broccoli, but Dora did. And so did I.

In the fall, I took her to look at the Dusky Canada Geese that would come to winter at the wildlife preserve just a few miles out of town. We just sat in the car and watched the v-lines of geese come in and land, watching how they grazed together on the tall green grass that covered the meadows around the small ponds on the preserve. She was quiet as I drove her home and I thought she hadn't been much interested in the birds. But the next day, Lilith told me she had described the geese in detail when asked what we did together.

I never talked to Dora about the her younger sister, but I think she had a healthy way of working through it in her little child's mind. One summer day when I was staying with Lilith, we heard Dora with the two neighbor girls, who were her best friends, playing with the Barbie dolls in the courtyard. Instead of having a wedding, they were having a funeral. They solemnly buried the dolls one by one and said good words over each. The next day they wanted to play with the Barbie dolls again and they were in the courtyard digging everywhere. They couldn't remember where they'd buried them. I guess they forgot the part about tombstones.

8 FIRE

There was a group of ladies who came to Lilith's house to quilt. When there was a quilt to be finished by the group, they would meet in her sewing room of her big house and work on it together. I already knew some of these ladies because they were friends that carried over and those few would often be at Lilith's house when I was visiting. There were two women from Eugene who were quilters and close friends.

When we heard that the book, *The Quilters: Women and Domestic Art* had been made into a play and a Portland company had scheduled a performance, we had to get tickets. Lilith, myself, and two other friends drove up to Portland to see it.

The story revolves around a group of pioneer prairie women and the stories that are stitched into the fabric of a quilt. Each of the characters had a story to tell and a different quilt that had special meaning because of something that happened in their lives while that quilt was being made. The stories were each different, some funny, some loving, some tragic.

There was the young girl who hated to sew. She and her sister were both learning to quilt with the classic child's pattern, Sunbonnet Sue. It is a simple block with a silhouette of a little girl in a prairie dress and a sunbonnet hiding her face. One of the little girls made a lovely quilt with Sunbonnet Sue holding a special object in each block. In her sister's quilt, she held a flower in one block, in another she held a gardening trowel, and so on. Then with a flourish, our tomboy revealed her version of Sunbonnet Sue. In each block was her depiction of the way she would like to murder Sunbonnet Sue. In one, she had a knife through the heart, in another it was a pistol shot that did her in. There were twelve ways to die on the twelve blocks. Her sister fainted straight away!

Each story was taken from a personal account of a pioneer woman and celebrated their contribution to the settling of the west. The four of us sat engrossed in the stories, proud to be carrying on the tradition. Lilith and I sat in the middle of the front row with our two friends on either side of us. We were enjoying each of the stories about the pioneer women and girls. Then came the scene about the girl caught in the prairie fire. She saw it from a distance at her cabin door and hoped her family would make it home soon. Then it got closer and closer, until she knew she must run to escape it. But prairie fires spread fast and soon she was surrounded by fire with no place to go. All three of us instinctively turned toward Lilith. She had begun to cry and we all leaned over and put our arms around her. The actors and the audience must have thought those four ladies in the front row were crazy; crying like that and holding onto each other!

After the show, the actors lingered to talk to people, as they often do in small theaters. Lilith went straight up to the actress that had done the fire scene.

"You made me cry and I just wanted to tell you it was alright."

"Oh, I am sorry, but it was a true story."

"Yes, you were wonderful. I cried because I lost a child by fire. It wasn't a bad thing. It was good to cry and you helped me to feel better."

What a wonderful woman! You gotta love someone like that, who can see through her own pain and thank someone for helping her let it go a little. Some of the most beautiful people I know have endured great tragedies. It's what makes them able to be so emotionally available to others. I guess you lose your fear of other people's emotions, once you've survived a personal tragedy of your own. For some people tragedy destroys all the beauty in life. They bottle up their feelings and shrivel up inside. But for others it opens a door. Lilith was an open door.

9 SCOTLAND

Betty's youngest son was on his own. The weaver's shop she was managing in Los Angeles was closing and her house in Hollywood was robbed twice. The second time, the owner arranged to have bars put on the windows. That was the last straw. It was a time for change. She had friends living in Scotland, now was the time to make that change.

The first year, she rented a house in Wales. After that she found a house in the Scottish Midlands. We had stayed in touch by mail ever since I left Los Angeles and I was following her adventure. She was a wonderful writer and one of the few people who, like me, enjoyed writing letters. There were beautiful descriptions of the countryside and the people she met. She described the accents and the culture in a way that made me want to be there. These were no tourist diaries, but stories of real life in Scotland. The letters often had small sketches to go with the descriptions and I saved every one of them. Later, when I went to visit her, I found that she had saved my letters, too. When she found out I had all of hers, she wanted copies. Somewhere, among her son's papers, I hope that correspondence still exists.

All those wonderful historical biographies we have today could never have been written if people hadn't kept diaries and written letters. In the past, people saved letters. They knew they were important. Sadly, today letter writing has mostly become a thing of the past. Few people write letters and an e-mail is seldom the same quality of writing as a letter. I wonder what historians will do in the future? You can't make an interesting biography based only on official documents. Can you imagine a twitter diary? It might be funny, but it would never be a literary master piece, or to my mind, in the category of a good read.

***

Betty's letters were a lot like the conversations we had. We talked about our lives, but we talked about things that were important to us; about nature, about things we'd made, artists we admired, and books we'd read. She often told me about books I would later read that have stayed on my short list of best books read to this day. She introduced me to Loren Eiseley because she said the way I viewed the world was a lot like his view. And *Shogun* by James Clavell is to this day, one of the best epic novels I have ever read. Both books changed the way I thought about writing. One a nonfiction, the other historical fiction.

I always thought the title of Loren Eiseley's book, *All the Strange Hours*, described exactly what an autobiography should be. After all, it's not the mundane things in life that make a story; it's the strange things. I promised myself that if I ever wrote my story, I would write about all the strange things. As it turns out, there have been more strange things than I could ever imagine. Eiseley is best known for his first book, *The Immense Journey*. It is notable for his original thoughts on human evolution, which predate the discoveries at Olduvai Gorge. This book marks him out as the first author of scientific books that appeal to the public. I didn't know this at the time; I just knew I was reading a book by a man who was a keen observer of human behavior and yet, somehow quite alone.

Betty was an insightful person. She knew I would be drawn to that book and she knew why. As I read the biographical information that is now available about Eiseley, I can see how, in many ways, his journey has been like mine. What Betty was trying to tell me was that there are some people who are meant to be alone and it might be a comfort for me to know there were others like me. She didn't mean literally alone, she meant a person with a lonely soul. Eiseley was married and had children. But in his personal and professional life, his thoughts were much more introspective than the average person. He used that personality trait, his intelligence, and creativity to become a unique and well respected scholar; even though he wasn't a person who fit in. I haven't done as well with my life, but certainly, I've learned that I'd best pursue my own talents and abilities because I will never fit into anyone else's normal.

Just before I made the decision to return to college in my thirties, my employer told me,

"You're not in the mold; go and find what fits you."

It was good advice; he knew my decision to take that risk was the right one. I had gone as far as I could go in that structured environment.

I've done my best to accomplish this, if not successfully. Leonard Cohen, another writer I admire, wrote,

"Like a bird on a wire, like a drunk in a midnight fire; I have tried in my way to be free."

I hope at least some of those who gave up on me or saw me as a failure will forgive me someday.

As for Clavell, he was my introduction to the epic historical novel. One can argue about the cultural accuracy of the novel, but in reality, history can only tell you so much. It was the colorful descriptions and details that brought the time period to life, as well as his imaginative character development, along with a spellbinding plot that made that novel great

***

Each visit with Betty was a new experience as we gradually grew closer. She taught me about tea and herbs, fiber and natural dying, and a different way of life. It was a way of life that paid attention to the beauty of everyday things and thus we were both also fans of the Arts and Crafts Movement of the early 20th Century.

This way of seeing the importance of the visual was what made her descriptions of life in Scotland so compelling. When the opportunity came to visit her in Scotland, I took it. It was my first trip abroad and I took three weeks. We walked the rolling hillsides of the Midlands countryside and stopped to watch the farmers bringing in hay in great round bales. We collected locks of sheep's wool that had drifted onto the fence wires, and we greeted the riders on horseback practicing for the Rideout.

The Rideout is a reenactment of the custom of patrolling the border between Scotland and England in the old days when the English were seen as invaders. In other words, they would literally ride out to patrol the borders. Patrols from each town would share the responsibility of patrolling a section of the border. They might engage a small group of soldiers scouting for a weak border entry or ride to warn the towns if an invading army was coming. Many times during my visit, I was told stories of the old days and of the heroic acts of Scottish fighters. The Scottish are part of the United Kingdom, but they never forget that they are Scots.

Politics have changed in Scotland since those days. At the time, they were getting ready for the elections in the UK, but the turnout was often poor in Scotland. Since everything was decided on popular vote, issues that affected the sparsely populated area of Scotland got little attention. As one of the neighbors put it while we were chatting at a Saturday Coffee Morning,

" We have to keep our priorities straight. The Rideout is more important than the elections."

So much of what I learned in Scotland was about history. There was an old Roman built bridge just outside the town where Betty lived where the surrounding area was rumored to be an old Roman soldiers' grave yard. It was said that you could sometimes see a soldier wandering the hillside near the bridge, but he would be walking knee deep in the heather, because the level of the hillside had risen since those old days. So, he still walked on the ground as he knew it in his time. Then everybody would laugh, irony was not lost in the telling of the tale. There were lots of these improbable stories that challenged belief in ghosts and other superstitions, yet gave credence to them at the same time.

There was a small river running under that old Roman bridge and I enjoyed doing my morning run along the river. It was the first time I'd ever run on a grassy riverside and it was a totally different experience to be near the water and the trees, with a light breeze blowing and the birds singing. It's just one more thing that was a pleasant surprise in Scotland. There are foot paths all over the countryside and you are free to follow them as you please, as long as you don't scare the cattle. There are actually turnstiles where the paths cut through pastures. So, you can go through without letting the animals out. So, much more friendly than in American farmland. In Scotland, the farmer will probably wave to you as you cut across his pasture; whereas, an American farmer might come out of his house with a gun. Oops!

**

Betty didn't have a car but her friends, Jake and Helen took us into Edinburgh one day to show us around. It was the most unique tour I've ever been on. We would be driving along and they would pull the car over in front of a bank or other imposing building, and Jake would say,

"We'll wait right here. Just run into that building and have a look at the ceiling and come back. There's a man in there who will give you a brochure."

Sure enough, the ceiling would be amazing, covered with hammered copper or a beautiful mural. And always, the man at the door would give me a brochure. It's really true policemen, and even security guards, are friendly all over the U.K.

We ladies, took a short shopping trip along a street of restored historic buildings, now used as boutique shops, while Jake ran around and did some errands. In a shop run by the Ladies Self-Aid Society there were handmade sweaters that I could afford. I got one for myself and one for my friend Joanne. We were the same size and she was the only shopping friend I've ever had. So, I had to bring back something fabulous for her. At lunch we stopped at another church with a coffee morning for a farmers' lunch of soup, homemade bread, and cheese.

My favorite stop was at the castle. We weren't going on the tour, but we were stopping in for the view from the parking lot. Jake and Helen smiled to each other. Helen winked.

"They charge to park, but watch this, they won't charge us."

Jake rolled down the window to talk to guard at the gate.

"I have a couple of friends here from America and I just want to take them right over there so they can have a look out over the city, whilst I tell them a wee story about Scotland."

The guard smiled and waved us through.

"Did you see how he puffed up when he mentioned the story about Scotland. So proud!" Helen said.

And indeed he was, everybody was proud of Scotland.

Betty had also made friends with two retired nurses from England and they came to take us to their house one day. It was my first trip into the Scottish countryside. There were gentle green hills dotted with sheep all along the way. At one intersection, we saw a row of dead rats attached to the fence in front of a pasture. When I asked why anyone would do such a thing, they told me that was the way the rat catcher got paid. He posted the rats he'd killed on the fence and the farmer would pay him per dead rat. I'd heard of rat catchers, but we don't have them in America, so this was an unusual bit of trivia for me.

The two ladies had a nice little two bedroom cottage on an old estate. As the golden days of the aristocracy were over, the gate keeper's house was for let and they'd been lucky enough to get it. Having been a large estate, the gate house was out of sight of the main house and surrounded by lawn and trees, with a small garden in the back. The only change they'd had to make was to enclose the garden for the two cats, They had been city cats and not wise in country ways, so had fallen prey to a local fox who saw them as invaders. So, the garden became their safe play area.

I sat and listened, to this story and more, fascinated, yet again, at the different accents. In this case, I could understand every word. Strange how English speakers the world over can understand an English accent, while we have to adapt to English accents from other regions.

10 LADIES AUXILIARY LUNCHEON

A few days later, Betty managed to get me added to a Ladies Auxiliary Tour to the Lake District. It's a beautiful area and one not to miss if you are traveling near there on the off season, though I've heard that large crowds can spoil the tranquil nature of that idyllic landscape during the high season.

My favorite part of the tour was tea time. Betty and I sat round a table with a group of ladies she knew best from the Ladies Auxiliary and ordered up a big pot of tea, crumpets, and scones.

"Oh, we've been calling them English Muffins in America. I wonder why. Wouldn't crumpet do just as well?"

Tea in America has no ceremony. It's served as any other beverage, sometimes including a snack. It can also be a regular part of a meal; just like coffee it may be served throughout the meal, and usually at the end of an evening gathering. That's the extent of it. I'd had high tea at a posh hotel once in Victoria, British Columbia. So, I knew it could often include sandwiches, as well as sweets; basically a full meal. I never experienced that in Scotland; it was a little different every time, but always fairly casual.

At tea and luncheon on the tour there was lots of chatting about the lovely scenery and of course, some talk about Beatrix Potter's house, her life, and work. It was mainly due to her efforts to buy up land and preserve it that we can still enjoy the Lake District today, much as it was in the early twentieth century.

On this day, when the tea arrived, whoever said, "I'll be mother," would serve. I didn't find out until years later, that at a formal tea, being invited to serve is an honor. "I'll be Mother," seemed more comfortable and friendly.

After the tour, Betty and I were also invited to the Ladies Auxiliary Luncheon the following week. It was a chance to meet more of the local ladies, since some of the older members were not able to go on the tour. When I arrived, I was treated as an honored guest; seated on the right of eldest member at the head of the table, with the youngest member on her left. These two ladies was so nice, showing interest in me and what life in America was like. I tried to make my responses interesting while also bringing the conversation around to Scotland. It went on pretty well at first. However, the elder lady had a very strong Scottish burr leaving me baffled, at times. I tried, "Excuse me, I didn't get that." "I beg your pardon, I missed something." "Sorry, what was that?" Finally, the younger lady realized what was happening stepping in to save me by literally translating what my hostess was saying. I felt embarrassed and also, worried that feelings might have been hurt; but truly I couldn't understand many of the words. Yet, I knew she was speaking English. This must be how foreigners to America feel upon meeting someone from the Deep South.

***

Betty had to go to the hospital for treatments once a week. I hadn't even known she was sick. She'd had a form of blood cancer for many years and the current treatment was to withdraw blood every week otherwise, her body produced too much blood. This was very much the way with Betty. She enjoyed life. It was precious. She didn't complain and she didn't make an issue of her health or other private matters.

She would be tired after her treatment, so I figured it was a good time to give her a rest from me, as well. After all, she was used to living alone. I wasn't sure how long she would be comfortable with a house guest.

I thought a day trip to the highlands would be just the thing. I went back to Edinburgh and took a Grey Line Tour. It was unique in its own way, too. There was no tour guide. The bus driver was a friendly sort and even stopped the bus once when he saw me trying to take a picture through the window. He gave all the scenic descriptions, and again there was a lot of pride in Scotland, even an occasional dig at England. One of the stories was about a castle that had been admired by Queen Victoria which she fancied having for herself.

"But the people of Scotland weren't of a mind to give it to her. Consequently, she went away in huff and never came back," he announced.

It was a weekday and the passengers were mainly people on their own for the day. This made conversation easy and we fell into pleasant conversation, laughing and joking all the while. Of course, one of the topics of discussion was where we were from.

One guy said, "I was born in Tipperary."

We all burst into song!

I stayed in an inexpensive bed and breakfast and as it turned out all the other tenants were cattle people who were there for the auction. Nice guys, a little rowdy, but polite. The maiden sister of the owners came and chatted with me after breakfast the next morning and asked about my travels. She shared her dream to go to India. It was on my dream list too and we had a good discussion about the places we wanted to visit. India was an important part of the British Empire for many years. You can still see the influence in the British cooking. To be honest, I had more curry while I was there than any other time in my life.

***

I went back to Oregon and continued my correspondence with Betty throughout the next year. She was having visa problems and eventually had to leave Scotland. It was a big disappointment for her. She had gone back to the US to visit family and when she reentered the UK, immigration noticed she'd overstayed her visa the last time. They held her at Heathrow Airport for thirteen hours before they finally allowed her to renew a one year visa. Can you imagine! What harm could an American pensioner do that would warrant holding her for that long? Sadly, this happens much more often these days. Traveling is still fun, but getting to your destination by flying is no longer part of the fun.

Betty's friends in Scotland were appalled at the treatment she'd received and they put her in touch with the local MP who tried to intercede on her behalf. She really wanted to stay in Scotland and she needed a long term visa. The appeal was rejected, but the MP advised her to appeal again and not to worry about overstaying the one year visa as long as she had an appeal in process.

To her shock and embarrassment, the local police came to find her, not at home, but at a friend's house while she was visiting. She was given a warning and a few days to leave without penalty. Her friends tried to convince her to continue trying for the appeal, but the humiliation was too much. So, you see these Visa problems are nothing new. The American passport may get you into more countries than most other passports, but it won't mean you are welcome to stay.

Betty returned to the United States and her brother found a house for her in a small town on the Oregon coast. She was able to get all her things out of storage, so she was comfortable and there was a small hospital where she could get her treatments.

I had returned to university in Eugene to complete my undergraduate work. I tried to get over to see her at least once a month, since it was only about an hour drive over to the coast, .

For a while, things went along smoothly. She was able to do her craft work and she even had the big floor loom set up in the front room. The little ice cream freezer she had bought at auction many years ago was still working and she began packing it up with homemade treats for the holidays, as she used to. She was walking distance from the grocer and there was a volunteer car service for seniors that came to take her for her treatments at the hospital. The volunteers were mostly retired people who were still active and had cars. The lady who drove her said she did it because she was glad to be able to help and would hope someone would do the same for her if she ever needed it. She became friends with the driver and her husband. They would often stop off at the drivers' home to spend time in the garden or have coffee while watching the rain, as one often does in Oregon. The climate was very similar to Scotland.

I felt happy that Betty was settled in near me and looked forward to our visits. I was studying Art History and I could talk to Betty about what I was learning. She knew all the artists and we shared our opinions about the different styles and periods.

One weekend we had planned a trip up the coast to see a friend of hers from Los Angeles who was there doing costumes on a film shoot. But the day before the trip, she called to say she couldn't make it. She was in the hospital. Betty's treatments weren't working and the doctors were trying to see if they could make adjustments to allow her to continue living a normal life. She would call her friend and make arrangements for me to still be allowed to visit the film location. She knew I was taking costume classes and was interested in costuming, as well as art history.

Of course, I didn't go to the film shoot. I went to the hospital to see Betty. She was apologetic for spoiling our trip.

"Never mind that, I said, "This is our time together and it doesn't matter that it is in the hospital instead of at the beach. Our time together is more important."

I read to her for a while from one of the British murder mysteries she loved. She would close her eyes and I would think she had drifted off.

Then she would quietly say, "Keep reading. I'm still listening."

After a while the nurses started coming by and peeking in to listen. They seemed to be enjoying it and one of them asked for the author's name and the title. It was a nice afternoon as hospital visits go.

Eventually the nurses said, I had to go. So, I headed back to the campus, sure they would have her treatments adjusted and she'd be home by the next time I came to visit.

She stayed in the hospital for a couple of weeks. Her foster daughter came up from Bakersfield and stayed a few days and her son Mark came from Santa Barbara one weekend. But they had lives of their own and they couldn't stay indefinitely.

They finally let Betty go home; this time it was for good.

There would be no more treatment, just some medication to make her comfortable. The cancer was not going to go away this time. It was summer time by then, so I was able to drive over once to see Betty and came back very upset.

I was staying at Lilith's house in Jefferson and I cried on her shoulder and told her the story when I got home.

"Betty is dying, I said, "She asked me to stay and take care of her, but I couldn't do that without dropping out of university. She's angry with me and says I'm putting my education before our friendship. That hurts me so much. It's my only chance to get a college education after being held back for years. She's asking me to make the sacrifice that even her family can't make. I am so afraid she is going to die being angry with me."

Lilith had lived through this pain before. I was so lucky to have her there for me.

"She isn't really angry with you. People just get angry because their loved ones are going to go on living, while they know they have to die."

This was hard, but I at least I wasn't alone. Lilith was one of those special friends who saw me through good times and bad. Our lives have gone in different directions, but she was there for me at the right time, when having someone like her in my life was most important. In that, life gave me a small kindness when I needed it most. Now, university life was ending. It was time to move on.

11 COLUMBIA RIVER GORGE

I passed Multnomah Falls, overlooking the Columbia River near the northwest corner of Mount Hood National Forest. I didn't stop there; I was looking forward to what I hadn't seen. It was early summer and the Columbia Gorge stretched out before me, a long blue ribbon bordered in green. For the first time in my life, I was flying down the highway solo; no one to rush me to the next town or gasoline station; no watching the gas gauge going down as another driver played chicken with the pit stops. No sleeping in rest stops because it was too late to find lodgings. I allowed myself five days to get to my destination, with a side trip to Yellowstone National Park. There was time to see things, do things, and with luck meet some interesting people.

Once at my destination, I knew it was going to be a long grueling season of summer stock with long hours and lots of backstage drama. The trip was all mine. It was going to be a sweet pleasure and possibly a once in a lifetime road trip.

I love driving with the windows down and a beautiful blue sky ahead of me. I like the scenery, watching the other vehicles going past in both directions and imagining who the people are and where they might be going. Some trips it's all recreational vehicles and wishing you could see the scenery. Others, it's mostly you and the truckers and you can pace yourself by whether they are breaking the speed limit or not. When the weather is really good, there are lots of motorcycles and memories of some good trips on winding country roads.

This was the first scenic section of the trip before I had to turn north and drive through eastern Washington, where it would be flat, hot, and dry all the way to Boise. It was gradually uphill and I wasn't worried about the heat or strain on the engine. Then I saw steam coming out of the hood, heard an explosion, looked down at the thermostat and it was red lining. I pulled over, got out and slowly lifted the hood. When the steam cleared, I found the radiator cap wedged between the back of the engine and the firewall.

I should have been watching the gauge more closely. But it hadn't seemed like a long steep climb. Grapevine Hill is a steep climb; that's a place where you watch your gauges carefully and carry extra water, just in case. In fact, Grapevine Hill is a bit of a legend.

This was a long narrow gorge with a slow climb; unlike Grape Vine Hill, which is a steep five mile climb over the Tehachapi Pass on I-5 between the Santa Clara Valley and The San Joaquin Valley. This wasn't like that; it was relaxing, the river on one side and the gorge wall on the other. But in the end, it wouldn't have mattered if I had watched the gauge, what happened was inevitable. But as one of my partners in crime used to say,

"It's all part of the adventure."

Breaking down when you are not near a town is always a sketchy situation. You don't know how long you will be on the side of the road and whether it's safe or not. They say you should stay inside the car. That's if you don't pass out from heat stroke in the summer. I remember one time, I had a flat in the middle of summer on I-95 in South Carolina. There was no phone signal and it was hotter than hell. So, I got a blanket out of the car and sat on the grassy shoulder until the highway patrol or some good citizen came along. It wasn't long before a patrol car pulled up. The patrolman got out of his car, took one look at me and with an accent like the warden in *Cool Hand Luke* said,

"Was you takin' a *suhn* bath?"

He actually said it just like that; *suhn*, pause, bath.

But I was in Oregon this time and I had a phone signal. I only had to talk to one flaky hippie before a tow truck came. Now I'm not opposed to hippies in general, and I've even been called one myself from time to time. It's just those certain ones who are all peace 'n love, dumb as a door knob, and still think they were put on earth to take care of all the women.

"Oh, I think you can go ahead and drive it to the gas station and just put more water in the radiator.

It was obvious that he knew nothing about cars. I'm no mechanic myself, but my dad was a pretty good mechanic and I learned the basics by watching and listening. It could be miles before the next place with a mechanic.

"It's ok. I have a tow on the way," I said as politely as I could.

I think he understood I wasn't looking for company.

I was just far enough from Portland that there were no major towns close by. I was near an exit, though and the tow truck took me to a wide place in the road that had a tavern, a motel, a grocery store, and luckily a service station with a qualified road mechanic. I was hoping to hang out for a couple of hours and be on my way. Bad news comes in threes and this was the second bad news that day. I had a blown head gasket and it wouldn't be fixed until the next day.

The mechanic assured me I could drive it down to the motel a block away to unload my baggage. The damage was already done, so I suppose driving two blocks wasn't going to matter. It was packed to the gills with suitcases and boxes that accounted for all the worldly possessions I couldn't bear to part with. And now one of my extra days was used up.

I pulled up to my motel room, opened the door and commenced to throw everything into the room. I'd noticed an unusual number of motorcycles in town and recognized the Hells Angels colors. There were a couple of them standing in the doorway of the next room watching my unseemly arrival. They didn't offer to help, just stared. I recognized one of them from one of the films the Angels had appeared in. The other one said,

"Was it a man?"

I stopped for a second and just looked at him.

"No, my car is broke down and I wasn't planning to stop here."

An overnight stay turned into two, guess there had to be bad news number three. But it gave me a chance to get to know my disreputable neighbors before I left. The Angels were having their annual gathering in a state park across the river. I talked to a few of them; they are actually pretty nice to strangers. I wasn't asking to join up though. They were on their best behavior, given that the Oregon State Police, the Washington State Police, the county sheriffs from both counties and the local police were out in full force. This was a time when the membership was starting to include lawyers and other professionals and the club was seeking to change its image. However my neighbors were somewhat discouraged by the public's unwillingness to accept their new respectability and their continued difficulty finding a place for their annual gathering.

The mechanic turned out to know his business and I kept that car for a couple of years more. But this was end of my tourist adventure for this trip. I knew I had to drive straight through now. I would have to make only pit stops and rest stops when I couldn't keep my eyes open any longer. Now I didn't just watch the truckers. I followed them. I slowed down when they slowed down, sped up when they sped up, and stayed close enough to the last truck in a convoy to hide from radar.

The truckers knew I was following then and noticed that I respected the unwritten rules; like don't get in front of them on a hill and don't get in between trucks that are trying to stay together. Eventually, they got curious about me. And one evening when I stopped for dinner at a truck stop one of them stopped to talk to me.

At first, I thought I was in for it. Not only had I been following them I was parking in the truckers' areas at the truck stops. They don't like that, in fact, in some rest areas it was against the rules. I didn't have to worry. They already had it figured out. They could see I was a woman traveling alone and knew I was doing it to feel safe. He asked me where I was going and what my situation was. By the end of the conversation, he'd offered for himself and his buddy to look out for me as long as I was headed their way. He told me to stay between his truck and his buddy's and they would ferry me until they turned south toward Denver. They call this the *rocking chair position* because you can just relax and drive. The truck in front watches out for trouble up ahead and the truck in back watches for patrol cars coming up from behind. Plus, you are pretty much shielded for radar; you're a small target between those two big diesels. That was back when radar was how you got caught.

The rest of this leg of the trip was pit stops, diner food, and cattle ranges where there was enough grass for feed. As I got further east, the grasslands faded and the landscape changed to empty space and buttes rising out of nowhere; the only sign of civilization--the train headed back where I came from.

12 LOSING THE TETHER

Once you make a decision to live a life of constant travel, that tether that binds you to people starts to unravel. I admit my ties that bind were pretty weak anyway. I was a delinquent runaway at age seventeen, divorced in my thirties, lost my house and went back to college shortly after.

I had a pretty stable support group of friends until I started working in theater. Once I went on the road, those friends fell away one by one. That day when my car broke down in the Columbia Gorge, I could hear it in my best friend's voice when I called her to let her know what happened.

"Are you still going to go?"

"I'm going if I have to take a bus to get there."

That was the last I ever heard from her.

I could hear Linda Ronstadt singing in my head.

"Everybody loves a winner: but when you lose, you lose alone." Deep down I knew she was already seeing me as a loser. With no job and no money, I was no longer the strong abandoned woman putting herself through college, brave and alone. Employers weren't impressed and friends were let down. Where was the success I was supposed to have become?

But in theater, they don't care who you are. They just care if you can show up and get the job done. I didn't have much time to think about it then. I just had to drive. During those years, driving saved me a lot of times from sinking into a total morass of depression. No time to think about loneliness, just survive.

And I was surviving; I had chosen a college major that had zero financial value. The current mantra was, *Do what you love, the money will come.* It would have been better to have a caveat, *But don't forget, life isn't fair.* Ironically, the one area that everyone agreed had less potential than my chosen major was theater. After one failed office job in Portland, the next job I landed was with a local professional theater.

I had worked in the costume shop in college and even designed a show, but the regional theaters were spread out across the country. I figured I couldn't even afford to go on interviews. How I worked in the Theater Department for three years and never found out that wasn't the way things worked is beyond me. But it never came up.

One night when hanging around at an after-party with the crew of Portland Stage Company, (now apparently defunct) the assistant stage manager announced she had landed a job in Germany. My jaw dropped! How had she done that? Everybody was shocked that I didn't know there was a trade publication where hundreds of theater jobs were advertised every month. Still thick headed, I asked,

"But how can you manage all those out of town interviews"

I earned my laughs here. Miracle of miracles, they did phone interviews. A month later I was on the road headed for Minnesota.

Here I was, Assistant Costume Shop Manager, on my second theater assignment, a good start and a learning experience. The intense schedule and mass production required for the big musicals that are summer stock's bread and butter breaks in many a young theater person. It can make or break you right out of the gate. I had the advantage of maturity that allowed me to be able to stay calm under a workload that sometimes seemed insurmountable. I had also been sewing since the age of nine. With that experience and the training I'd gotten in the university costume shop, I was in my element. Corset? No problem! Codpiece? You've got it! 1920s flapper dresses? A walk in the park!

What I wasn't ready for was that there would be more drama behind the scenes than on stage. Tantrums by 'wanna be' leading men and women. Costume fitters that behaved inappropriately. And sex as the main off stage entertainment. I could ignore it as long as it didn't affect the shop. But these things have a way of spilling over and affecting everybody in the cast and crew.

That summer job got my foot in the door. But I left two weeks early to avoid being a witness in an ethics committee investigation of the theater's employment practices. Like many people in the business, I thought I would get black balled from theater, if I told what I knew. It's not like that.

I had arranged to visit my mother at the end of the season. So, I headed toward St. Louis. I guess it's in my nature to hit and run. But I always feel better once I'm on the road. The road is now. The past is literally behind you and anything can happen.

It was late July by that time, It was hot and muggy in the Midwest and I got caught in a downpour in a small town in the Wisconsin Dells; its name I never learned. There was a hotel with a no vacancy sign and one motel. The motel manager at first said they were full. After asking after other places I could go, they realized there was no other place, and I could not go further in this storm. I would likely be sitting out the storm in their parking lot. They had a room that needed work on the shower but said I could stay there if I didn't mind. I didn't. I just wanted a place to dry out and rest. They didn't charge me much, since they weren't planning on renting that room until after the plumber came. It wasn't too bad; old and run down like the rest of the town, but clean with a shower that just kind of drizzled.

The next day I headed south through more mid-west farmland. Just before Beloit, I saw a sign – "Mexican Restaurant 3 miles." Mexican restaurants weren't that common in the Midwest at that time and it was nearly lunch time. So, I turned off the main highway expecting to find one of those restaurants that are so often next to a gas station near a highway. But the road narrowed just a mile or so past the off ramp and at three miles there was a nicely kept building with a dirt parking lot. Aah! Mexican food! I missed the west coast.

I was dressed for the road, not as a tourist. But I realized as I walked into the restaurant, I didn't look like a Mid-westerner. My hair was braided and I had put on a loose peasant blouse and a big skirt. I hate how shorts ride up at the crotch when you sit in the car for a long time. A skirt and a loose blouse is much cooler. But now I realized this was exactly the kind of skirt Frida Kahlo wore in her many self portraits. The wife of Diego Rivera and child of a Mexican mother and German father, she became known as the most Mexican of all Mexican women. A full circle skirt in three layers of gathered panels, big earrings and a bracelet of Mexican silver and lapis lazuli finished my outfit. I hesitated a moment; did I look like a wanna be Mexican?

There was no one else in the restaurant and the three employees stopped talking and stared when I walked in. They were Mexican, and I was obviously not; but I was unintentionally dressed like one. They were quiet people and there was no verbal harassment, like I might have gotten in L.A.

I seldom stop in a restaurant when I'm on a road trip. I usually just keep up my energy with caffeine and carbohydrates from convenience stores and make up for it when I reach my destination. So, I was hungry and I ordered a full carne asada dinner. This was authentic Mexican food, not Tex-Mex or California style. It was the best Mexican meal I have ever eaten.

I could probably never find that restaurant again, if it still exists. It was surrounded by farms and not visible from the highway. There were just the two signs and the distance to guide you there. It was a nice surprise, but not unbelievable. Lots of Mexicans come to Minnesota, Iowa, and Wisconsin during harvest season. In Minnesota, the State encourages them to stay by having liberal welfare benefits and housing. They want to keep the best workers there for the next harvest season. If they have to go back home or stay and live illegally there is a good chance they won't make it back for the next season. I'll never know these people's true circumstance, but in my imagination, this was a family that came north, worked in the fields, maybe even cooked for the summer workers, saved their money and eventually opened a restaurant. They had a business and I had a great meal in a place far from any fancy restaurants with stars behind their names. It was a fair exchange in my book.

I wonder what story they made up about me after I left.

13 THE EAST COAST

It was a whole new culture; different accents, different social culture, and different food; all added up to a major change for me. I had returned to Portland with my twelve year old car, wondering if it would survive a 3,000 mile trip. Not only that I was almost flat broke. But I had a job. If I could just get there, I could survive.

I negotiated with the theater to reimburse me for travel as soon as I arrived. I just needed enough money to live until the first pay day. The car would have to go. It should have been simple; put an ad in the local paper and wait for responses. Somehow life is never simple. A couple of people drove by and looked, but their budgets were for a garage sale. I hate selling used stuff. It doesn't matter what it is, it can be a used car or a complete set of Dam dolls. Whatever you are asking for they want it for next to nothing. If you list a car that runs for a hundred dollars, they will want it for five.

On the second day, I got a call from a guy in a bar. He would pay cash if had all my service receipts and it was in the condition advertised. This was a little sketchy. No, it was really suspicious! But he was the first person who had called that actually had money. What was the catch? I had to bring it to him.

I found the bar in a strip mall on the outskirts of the city. It seemed a little out of the way for a guy without a car. But he and his friend were waiting for me when I arrived and seemed mostly sober. They did a thorough check of the inside and out and did a quick perusal under the hood. I don't think either of them knew much about engines, but with guys, it's kind of obligatory. They think they have to look at the engine. It's a guy thing.

Personally, I've only met one guy who didn't have a hang up about cars.

I've known several who had sports cars in pieces on the garage floor. But this one guy, he was too smart to care about ego. He had a degree in engineering, but he spent most of his time repairing farm equipment. I don't mean puny little poor excuse for a tractor lawn mowers; I mean big equipment; windrowers, hay balers, combines, and any kind of field harvest equipment.

So, you might think he would be particular when he went to buy a truck. You'd be wrong. He knew the make and model he wanted; he walked into the dealer with his information and asked if they had any.

"We have two of those on the lot right now, a red one and a blue one."

"I'll take the blue one."

"Don't you want to test drive it first?"

"Does it run,"

" Yes"

"Then I don't need to test drive it."

That must have made the salesman's day. In and out in less than 30 minutes.

But I digress. My sale wasn't difficult either. The small time hustler liked that the car looked good for it's age. And he liked that the engine was rebuilt. Less chance of anything expensive breaking in the near future. But I don't think he was worried about what was going to happen in the next two years.

There was a back story. He had bet his friend fifty dollars he could have a car in less than an hour. Done deal!

They were headed out to Las Vegas, or as I like to call it, Lost Vegas. I was obviously alone.

"How are you going to get home?"

"Well, since I brought the car to you, I figured the least you could do was drop me off."

A disappointed look. These guys must have an appointment in Vegas. I was guessing the fifty dollar bet wasn't the only thing that went down with them that day. However they ended up in Portland, there was no sign of the transportation that brought them there. Whatever it was had probably paid off another bet and not too long ago. They would probably turn the odometer back and resell the car when they got to Vegas, but that wasn't my concern. I had cash and a job waiting for me. That's all I needed.

I was a little hesitant to give them the address where I was staying, but they did seem to be in a hurry to leave town, so I had them drop me right in front of the house. The better half was home when I got there, so I felt a little saver.

"So, did those guys buy the car."

"Yeah, I had to pick them up in a bar. But they had cash."

He laughed.

Goodbye, Portland, and the last friends I knew, for a long time. No car trip this time; I opted for AmTrack. It wasn't not much cheaper than flying, but they had baggage cars. When you are a costumer, you need stuff. AmTrack would allow me two full sized suitcases and two trunks at no extra charge. It was a three day trip and the dining car served chef cooked meals. This was AmTrak's last gasp effort at making trains a gentile form of travel. It had good food, friendly service, and an observation car. There was even informal entertainment. On one leg a park ranger came onboard and gave a little history and geology lesson about the national park we were passing through. On another leg, a magician went around to all the cars to entertain the children. Because of limited seating, passengers were seated at tables according to the number in their party. If your reservation was for less than four, you were seated with another small group. It made of good conversation and a chance to meet other passengers. We chatted and enjoyed the scenery at dinner every evening. It was totally relaxing, just what I needed before starting a new job.

Trains were losing long distance travelers and they were attempting to make them into a travel experience. Flying, would never be an experience.

There were no disasters on this trip. It was a relaxing ride with beautiful scenery. I spent several hours in the observation car up until Chicago and I got out and stretched my legs whenever there was a long stop during the day. The train turned into a commuter run from Chicago to Philadelphia, so no more fancy dining car or entertainment for the kids.

This is where the luxury ended. Someone peed on the bathroom floor within the first thirty minutes and there was a woman behind me with a crying baby. She just kept rocking the poor thing and saying,

"Shuddup," in a low growling voice.

I gave the theater a call when I arrived and asked for someone to pick me and my baggage up at the station. They knew right away that I was not an east coast person. When the shop manager asked which station, I said,

"Penn Station."

Luckily, 30th Street Station is the only AmTrak station in Philly. They were going to have to break me in.

In about an hour, the costume shop manager picked me up and we had time to get to know each other during the ride to the theater. She was born and raised in Pennsylvania and surprisingly liked country music. She was a little older than me and had gotten into the hippie scene when I was still in high school. I'm not sure what that was like in Pennsylvania, not like L. A., I'm sure. But when it started raining she did mention she had to concentrate because she got rainbow flashbacks from the rain on the windshield. I was hoping we would arrive safely. The scene shop manager did ask me how I enjoyed the drive when I met him the next day. I could tell there was a joke there somewhere, Apparently it was the first time my boss had ever driven a van and she'd never driven in Philly traffic before.

I had no idea how I was going to find a place to live, but the theater had promised to find me a place that would do at least temporarily. As it turned out, I would have a third floor room in a Victorian row house just three blocks from the theater. My host who was the Executive Director at the local symphony, had traveled all over the world; working first for the Peace Corps and later for a non-profit that was helping build schools and hospitals in Africa. He was a multi-talented artist and a man who understood people.

Anything could have happened, we'd never met before and the people at the theater didn't really know me. It was supposed to be just temporary, but I ended up staying there the whole season and he became one of my dearest friends. He has his own story, but that comes later.

This stop lasted nine months and it was an introduction to so many new things. It was my first time preparing costumes for up to eight persons on my own. It was my introduction to New York theatrical designers and equity players. New York City was an hour and a half away. So, I was able to visit world class art galleries and see artworks that I had only seen in slides while studying art history in college; and of course, there were the Broadway shows. When I had a free weekday between shows, I went to a matinee show of Jelly's Last Jam, choreographed by Gregory Hines, whom I adored.

But most important, it was the first time I had lots of gay friends and was able to see what their lives were really like. It was a time of change and confusion for them. It was the mid 1990s and the AIDS epidemic had already taken thousands of lives. The general public was just becoming aware that there was a significant gay population, and it was in shock. There was still a lot of prejudice, but more and more people were coming out of the closet because they knew, in this time of crisis, the only way to get through it was to band together.

It didn't take long for me to understand that they hurt just like anyone else when they lost their friends, their lovers, or their spouses. And there was a lot of hurt just then.

14 KEN

I loved living in that house. My room looked out on the row houses across the street and I could see the people coming and going in the neighborhood. I had my belongings shipped from Portland, so I had my own bed and a cedar chest full of quilts I'd made myself. My dress form stood in the tower window and the sewing machine was under the other window, where the light was good all day. I had the art books I'd collected over the years and the costume texts from pattern making classes. It felt like home.

Ken had the second floor with his bedroom in the back and office on the street side. All the rooms and the hallways were hung with his drawings and paintings and it was like reading a story as I followed the hallway down the two flights of stairs to the living room.

Once in awhile I would stop and have a short conversation with him in his office where he worked on the weekends. One day he began talking about his Peace Corps experience in India. His background was in public health and he had been sent there to oversee a project in a small village where they were bringing running water and electricity to all the homes. It was the nineteen sixties and they were still carrying water from the river and lighting their houses with kerosene lamps. He lived in the home of the village chief and as he began to tell the story of this family, he brought out a ream of paper. There was a photographic portrait of each family member; the mother and father, the son and his wife, and their first child. There was a biography of each person along with their portrait. It was a book he had been writing and like me, he'd let lie dormant for years.

It was an important story and one that needed to be told. It occurred at a time when India was on the cusp of changing from a totally traditional culture to one that was emerging into the twentieth century. The Peace Corp projects were to bring the benefits of the modern world that were most needed in the countryside to the people to ease the burden of poverty and allow the next generation to have choices that were never possible before. The parents were of the old generation. The father saw that electricity and running water would improve the lives of everyone in the village, but he did not want traditions to change. The wife still cooked all the meals and served the men before sitting down to eat.

The daughter-in-law did the laundry at the river each morning and this was where Ken got to know her. They had to be very careful about how and when they talked because of the social restrictions on a married woman. So, Ken would stand on the little bridge that crossed the river and look down and they could talk as she washed the clothes in the river below the bridge without causing any gossip. She knew the world was changing and she wanted to be a part of that change. But a married woman belonged, not only to her husband, but to the his family, as well. She must do her duty to her mother-in-law until the day she died. Then she would take over the responsibilities of the home. There was nothing else in her future.

Not much was said about her husband, but he must have been a traditionalist like his father. Perhaps he never knew of his wife's desire for an education, a chance to do something outside the home, or just simply to make her own choices rather than be a servant to the family. As Ken showed me the picture of this beautiful woman, his eyes welled up; she had taken her own life.

Ken passed away before the book was ever published and I lost track of his friends after the funeral. But his best friend took charge of managing his affairs. I hope he saw the value of that book and did something good with it.

It wasn't all serious. Ken cooked dinner every night. At first, I felt guilty, but eventually I realized he enjoyed it. I would just get in there and fix the salad or do the washing up. I hate washing up, but I had to do my part, Ken was such a wonderful cook. Even when I had guests over to the house, he'd come in after work, see me in the kitchen and take over. I might be starting the dinner prep with one of my friends and somehow he would always end up taking over the main dish. We would gradually be moved down the line and become the assistants. He was a natural born host.

I usually invited the visiting designers from New York over for dinner on one of the nights they were in town. They always stayed in a hotel and the home cooked meal was welcome. These were New York designers who had worked in television, movies, and opera, and taught at the universities with the best theater programs. They would take these out of town gigs because, even for New York, designers' work isn't steady and it was a welcome break from waiting for the next New York assignment.

I was just a working class woman who'd put herself through college after a messy divorce. I had traveled a bit around the United States because my father worked construction. But it was nothing like the lives these women had lead. We would talk a bit about the current show and some of the work they were doing in New York. When the conversation would lag, Ken would come to the rescue and the conversation would turn to what was currently happening in Africa, or the latest art show or event in New York. The conversation would just flow. This was a whole new world to me and one where I knew I didn't quite belong.

Ken was my introduction to the local community. He was active in the local non-profit AIDS awareness and assistance organization and I would help out with these events, as well. Until that time, I did not understand the gravity of the situation. Every one of his friends had lost someone to this epidemic. They were desperately trying to find a way to stop it, while they were dealing with their own grief and trying to put their shattered lives back together. Love knows no race or gender. We all feel it the same way, and we all suffer for it.

Mostly though, it was day to day living, the warmth of feeling accepted, and the security of feeling at home that I liked about living with Ken. Ken worked long hours at the symphony. Mine were shorter, but then there were the long hours during load in and dress rehearsals. But we still ate together, cleaned house together, and watched TV together. Our favorite program was Northern Exposure. I had the armchair and Ken would lay out his long fame on the big couch. Sometimes he would fall asleep before it was over. Usually, I would just turn off the TV and go quietly upstairs when it was over. But one night he woke up just as I was shutting it off and said,

"What happened?"

"You fell asleep."

"Why didn't you wake me?"

I had to think about this for a minute. My dad had been a tough construction worker who left every morning around five a.m. He hated getting up early and on weekends he slept in. There would be hell to pay if we kids woke him up with our noise before noon. He had a hot temper and we didn't want to feel the wrath of his belt. There was one time when I did wake him up though. A salesman had come to the door asking for "the man of the house." I was in my last year of high school and I was so flummoxed by this formal expression from a stranger, that I felt compelled to obey. I knocked softly at the bedroom door where he was only taking a nap.

"I couldn't be too bad," I mused to myself.

"Daddy, there's a man at the door asking for you."

He did get up. He walked straight to the front door wearing only his undershorts. "What can I do for you young man?"

The young man in question had apparently been selling some sort of baby furniture. He took one look at Dad, one at me and realized his mistake.

"Oh, excuse me, sir. I've made a mistake. I'm sure you aren't interested in cribs and bassinets."

And he was off. Dad and I looked at each other and burst out laughing! It was a college town and he'd apparently thought I was a young married student. These times were few and far between, but I guess that's why I remember it so well.

It was the fear that started my taboo against waking anyone. I retold the story to Ken and he just smiled.

"Don't worry. I won't get mad if you wake me."

From then on, it was my job to keep him awake through Northern Exposure. He'd start nodding off and I'd throw a pillow over there. He'd wake up and we'd both smile and go back to watching our show. That's what home should feel like.

***

Ken had a big Samoyed dog named Taz. He was a jumping, bouncing ball of fur that never got enough exercise. We were in a row house, so there was only a small back yard, not enough room for a dog that size to play. He got to come inside when we were home, especially when it was raining or snowing. He had a dog house, but being a northern dog, he didn't really feel the cold. Often times he would just stand on top of his house out in the rain or roll in the mud. It was just easier to bring him inside before he became bouncing ball of mud that would be flung all over the Indian carpet as soon as he could get to the living room.

He was well behaved, but didn't like to be alone. He knew when we were in the house and if we left him alone, he knew it. Occasionally, he would escape and run wild around town. The first time it happened Ken blamed himself. The next time he strongly questioned me, but I never went out the back way, so that didn't explain it. He questioned the neighbor kids, who liked to play with Taz through the fence; thinking they might have been tempted to open the gate to play with him in the back alley. Ken moved the gate latch higher, just in case. They couldn't reach it, so there would be no reason to question them if it happened again.

I love dogs and Taz and I became great friends shortly after I moved in. I tried taking him on my runs to give him more exercise, but that was a bad idea.

Ken said, "Oh, he's trained to stay with me in the park. You can let him off the leash as soon as you are away from the road and on the trail."

I tried it once. The moment he was off the leash he went charging ahead. That dog could run fast, way faster than me! Luckily, his love of people caused him to stop and try to socialize with the first family he met and I was able to retrieve him. I apologized and the family was nice about it. But

I had visions of less dog friendly people in my head.

I'd had an Alaskan Malamute a few years back. Their personalities are similar, but they are much bigger than Samoyeds and their mere size can frighten people. She took off running towards a guy practicing his golf swing in the park one day and he was set to swing at her with a nine iron. This time the dog returned on my call before she was swinging distance from the golf club. Ken would never forgive me if anything happened to Taz. So, that was the only time I took her to the park alone.

Ken wasn't traveling much at that time, but one weekend he and the guys went off to ski for the weekend. It was snowing and the ski season in Pennsylvania was short, so they were anxious to go. I had Taz to keep me company and everything went fine the first evening and the next day. But on Sunday after I went out on an errand, I opened the back door to find Taz was gone, again. Why, oh, why did this have to happen on my watch?

I was worried about leaving him outside alone, but I didn't want to leave him inside alone either. Dogs who don't live inside often panic when left inside the house alone. There can be a lot of damage done in a short time. A friend of mine left his Labrador Retriever in the garage one day, thinking the dog would be fine until he got home. The Lab jumped through the glass in the upper half of a side door and ran off. Crazy dog! He wasn't injured and came back all happy after about half an hour.

Taz tended to cover a lot of ground fast. I went all around the neighborhood calling him, but saw no sign of him. When I got home, Ken was there and he called the pound. Twice Taz had been found miles away and turned in at the pound. They didn't have him, but said they'd call him if anyone turned him in. Truant dog!

Ken got in the car and went out farther looking for him but found no sign of him. Later that day, he got a call from a family across town that had held onto him when he showed up to play with their dog. He was tagged with address and phone number, so they knew he was a lost dog. He was too far from home. Ken went over and retrieved him from the nice family.

We were glad to have him back, but mystified at how he had gotten out. It seemed there was no way to keep him in if he was determined. About a week later, Ken discovered the answer. He was looking out the window and noticed Taz standing on his hind legs at the gate. He watched him and in a minute Taz had lifted the latch and opened the gate. Caught red handed! After that the gate latch was changed to one that could only be opened from the outside. I wasn't tall enough to reach it, but I didn't need to go out the back any way. I told you he was a smart dog.

14 REVENGE

Yes, I hated the alligators. Including that lousy mascot. I hated that I couldn't go for a run on campus without watching out for the really big ones. You can't imagine how big they get until you see the ones that are growing in a preserve with no predators to keep them in check. I'd be running along past the lake and see a gator head just above the water about three feet long. That meant the body was anywhere from twelve to fifteen feet long and that didn't slow them down. They were fast. I'd cross the road hoping it wasn't hungry enough to chase me. Otherwise, I wouldn't stand a chance.

I lasted two years and left the year before my thesis presentation. I had already seen a lot of people come and go and I realized no one in professional theater cared about the degree. For actors, graduating from NYU or Yale graduate program meant something. For tech people there were very few universities that had respected programs. I was offered an internship at The Costume Collection in New York. And decided that would be my best option. I would be getting training and critiques from professionals within The Costume Collection, guest lectures from designers who were actively working in New York City, and have a design project overseen by a New York designer. It had been a whim, I wasn't getting encouragement from my faculty advisors, so I thought,

"Why not try?"

I'd not felt the critiques I was getting from the costume professor were objective and this would at least give me an objective critique.

There were only ten spots available and the competition was open to designers nationwide. The goal was to give opportunities to new designers who didn't have the advantage of living in New York to experience the New York theater scene. Therefore, the only restriction was that designers already living and working in New York were not eligible. The competition included a portfolio review and a phone interview with the finalists. The deadline passed and I had not heard the final results. They had promised that a letter would be sent informing me of their decision either way. Normally, no phone calls are accepted from applicants. So, I was hesitant to call, but I had to know!

As politely as I could, I called and introduced myself.

"I was one of the candidates for the internship and I haven't heard anything. I was just wondering if you've made your final choices."

The voice on the other end of the line wasn't angry!

"Yes, we have and you were one of our choices. We were wondering why we hadn't heard from you. Do you accept?"

"Of course, I wouldn't miss it for the world!"

The following week I had my annual review with the snooty costume professors who hadn't recommended me for the internship. The new professor, who had directed the main stage show I had designed hadn't hesitated to recommend me. He was from New York and he wasn't planning to stay in The Swamp indefinitely.

"Go to New York. That's where you have to be if you want to make it."

Back at the department review meeting, imagine their surprise when I didn't break down in tears when they told me that they didn't have a show for me the following year. I smiled and said that was no matter, I had been accepted for the New York internship and I wouldn't be back the following year.

But nature has a way of putting us in our place when we get a little too arrogant. I had made my announcement. I had endured their snide insults and I wasn't going to take any more. I closed my portfolio, stood up, and very seriously said,

"This interview is now over."

Portfolio over shoulder, I turned to go. What I hadn't noticed was that I had been sitting with my right ankle resting on my left knee the whole time and my leg had fallen asleep. So, my grand exit was a hobble. But I still didn't look back.

16 THE WEBSTER

No road trip this time. I was going to be in New York for the summer, so having a car was not practical. I flew into JFK and went straight to the boarding house where The Costume Collection had reserved rooms for the female interns at a historic women's hotel that had been built in 1923. The building was well maintained and public rooms had been remodeled over the years to make them more comfortable and convenient. But they had kept some interesting details from the early days.

There was a sewing room with a cutting table, a couple of sewing machines and even a dress mannequin on the second floor. There was a resident's garden outside the dining room and another garden on the roof. I felt really pampered to live in a place with gardens and a rooftop view right in the middle of Manhattan. There was a laundry with modern washers and dryers, a clothesline outside, and a drying room.

The drying room was one of those peculiar inventions from the early twentieth century. Most of the household appliances from that period have disappeared, because they have been replaced with things that are more reliable or the device just didn't work all that well in the first place. But the drying room fascinated me. The hot water heaters for kitchens and bathrooms, as well as the steam heat for the rooms were located on the roof. The huge hot water tanks and the many pipes needed to carry hot water throughout the hotel were enclosed in a room, out of sight of the lovely rooftop garden. Some clever person realized that a lot of heat was being lost and had installed drying racks next to the pipes. You opened the door to a big closet like room, pulled out a rack, hung your clothes on it, slid it back, and viola, your clothes got dry on a rainy day.

I wonder if the little sewing room and the drying room are still there? It was so convenient to be walking distance to just about anywhere you wanted to go in Manhattan and just a block from the subway for reaching the other boroughs.

The hotel was, at that time, operating as a non-profit hotel for single working women, who could stay up to five years. Sadly, it's since changed hands and is no longer a women's hotel. As far as I know, this is the end of an era. San Francisco had one hotel for women when I first moved there in 1994, but after a fire, it was remodeled and reopened as another venue.

I enjoyed my stay there—except for this one day. I got a note in my box to see the manager. What could she want? The Costume Collection had given a reference for us and I had no outstanding charges. What could be the issue? I entered the small office with only a large desk and some shelves in the corner. Sitting behind it was a woman who was the epitome of the expression, battle axe; late fifties, closely trimmed helmet hair, and a conservative suit pulled too tight over her ample bosom, and an expression that suggested I had committed a crime.

"You have only filled in the space for one emergency reference. We require two."

"That's because it's the only one I have."

"It's your mother, you say here. What about your father?"

"Dead, Ma'am."

"Well, we must have another reference. It's the rule."

This was starting to feel personal. I was recently divorced and not on the best of terms with my family. And I had been in theater just long enough to lose most of my non-theater friends and not long enough to make new ones. Besides which, I was in my forties, so about twenty years older than most of my colleagues.

"Alright you can put down my sister."

"And what is her address?"

"It's the same as my mother's. They live together."

The face grew darker.

"That won't do. We need two addresses."

This was getting a bit strange. Had she never heard of adult relatives who live together? What difference did it make if emergency contacts had the same address, as long as they were responsible adults?

One last try.

"I have a brother. He lives next door." I recited the address.

Silence.

"That's all I have." I said and turned to go.

My mind was already racing ahead. I would have to ask the Director of The Costume Collection to help me find emergency housing, and that would mean repeating this entire embarrassing situation. Older single women really are discriminated against.

It was three steps to the door and I had my hand on the door knob.

Slowly, "Alright, you can stay."

"Thank you." I said and without turning around went through the door.

I wanted to put this behind me and fast. The internship was not a vacation, I had a project to complete and I didn't want this weighing on my mind.

Looking back, I still wonder why I was singled out like that? Was she trying to get rid of me? What could possibly be gained by that. There were eight of us staying in the same hotel and I am sure they got a lot of theater and arts people living there. Were they that much in demand? Or was it just my age?

17 A CIRCUS LIFE

The internship ended and I was on the road again. I had found a position as a cutter in a shop near Baltimore. It was good work with a full team for each pattern maker and cutter. Now I got to see how much work a well oiled team can put out.

It was a good learning experience, but life always throws us a curve and this was another short lived assignment. This time it was the law that intervened. I had been so focused on just surviving that I hadn't kept track of things that I might have missed during all this moving around.

One morning on the way to work, I was stopped by the local police. My Florida plates had drawn attention and he'd noticed that they were expired. I hadn't. Then things got complicated. I had not lived in Maryland long enough to be a resident and therefore wasn't eligible for a Maryland driver's license or car registration. After several phone calls to Florida, I was at a dead end. There was no way I could renew my registration without coming to the Department of Motor Vehicles in person. There was no alternate transportation to the shop, since it was in the suburbs. I would have to go back to Florida.

It was another fourteen hour drive down the I-95. I was starting to hate that interstate. I drove straight through and arrived in Gainesville too late to go to the DMV. I slept in my car that night and the next and then swallowed my pride and called a friend from grad school. He had an extra room and I was welcome to stay a couple of nights. I knew it was going to take longer than that to find another job. But it was a couple of nights of shelter and a shower.

I bounced around from place to place for a while but eventually landed a position as a stitcher at Busch Gardens, Tampa. This was one of the most strange and wonderful places I would ever work. Busch Gardens, Tampa doesn't have the Clydesdale horses like the one in St. Louis, but it has a lot of variety for a small amusement park. There were the usual thrill rides, and walk around characters. It had three outdoor stages and an ice show in the indoor theater. Everyone had a uniform or a costume. Retail workers turned in their uniforms for laundering at an onsite laundry at the end of each shift. All the performers costumes came through the costume shop. They picked up their costumes in the morning and dropped them off for cleaning after their shift.

The shop did all the repairs, and all the new costumes were designed and created in the shop. There were eight of us, plus the Shop Manager, Assistant Shop Manager, and a half dozen on-call seamstresses who worked from home. There were no cutters or pattern makers. We were each assigned a set of costumes and we had to do them start to finish. We drafted our own patterns, cut each costume, did the sewing, attended fittings, and did alterations on all of our assigned pieces. I had to use every bit of my experience from my short time in theater.

The lively personalities on the costume crew made for a busy but fun environment. The best seamstress on the crew was a tiny Italian American lady in her sixties. Her mother had been a seamstress at one of the couture houses in Italy before she immigrated to the United States and she had taught her daughter everything she knew. She wouldn't partner with anyone, so much of what she knew was lost when she retired. However, I sat next to her which allowed me to see how she did things, on the sly.

In any case, it wasn't all sewing. We each took turns on check-in and check-out, which gave us a chance to meet all the players. There were musicians, skaters, and dancers. Then there were the people who wore the walk around character costumes, whose faces you never got to see in the park. And, then there was the snake dancer!

She would come in carrying a large sort of lumpy looking handbag and turn in her costume. One day she asked me to keep the bag while she went to the ladies room. My stomach was doing flip-flops just thinking about it.

"No, I couldn't do that."

"It's ok. He can't get out."

"Sorry."

I was imagining all the fabric stacked up on shelves by the cutting table. All of it wrapped on those long hollow cardboard tubes, not to mention all the other places a snake could hide in a costume shop. I told her she could leave it on the floor in the entryway where I could see it.

Of course, the costume crew was listening and couldn't wait to tell me another snake story when I got back to my station. Have you ever wondered how they manage the care and feeding of a snake that is going to be used on stage? You can train a dog or even a horse to behave politely on stage. But the fascination with the snake dancer is partly about the presence of an animal that can't be trained. They do not perform tricks. They are just reacting to the motion of the dancer.

So, how do they prepare them for the stage? Well, they have to massage them before each performance to – ahhm – relax them. Just once, this important task was not done with care. As the dancing lady began twirling around, the snake relaxed. The result not only sprayed all over the costume, but all over the audience as well. I'll bet that cured them of ever going to a snake show again!

There were other animals on the lot, too. In a way, it was more like a winter home for a circus than an amusement park. There were rides, live entertainment, carnival food, and even a small zoo.

We always joked about the different parts of the park. There were maps for the guests of course, but those did not include the back lot roads and rear entrances. Their layout could be confusing, so if I had to go on an errand the other crew members would give directions depending the areas of the park and where the back entrances were.

They'd say, " Follow the back pathway until you see the entrance on the right with the carnival tent."

Or, "Go past the roller coaster, you can see it over the wall. Then enter when you see the jungle bridge."

For some reason, the theater with the ice show was near the entrance to Gorilla Land.

So, they'd say. "Take the pathway on the right and don't go through the mist; never go through the mist."

There was a fake mist at the entrance to Gorilla Land.

I had to see the gorillas, so on my day off; I went through the mist. There was a small band of gorillas in a lush enclosure with an outdoor viewing area and a glassed in underground area where you could sit quietly and just observe for a while. It was early, just after the park opened, so there were not many visitors. At first I was the only one in the gorilla enclosure. I could see the gorillas wandering around, lying on the rocks, or eating the plants that grew in the enclosure. They had other food provided by their keepers, of course, but they still liked to browse. After a few minutes a caretaker with a clip board came and took a seat on a bench in the corner. She would observe the activities of the small troop and occasionally make a note.

As time passed, the park became more active and more visitors arrived. The next visitors were a group of teenagers. They stopped at the outside observation platform and almost immediately one of the boys started shouting and waving to the gorillas. Of course, the male began making aggressive gestures. Encouraged by the squeals of the girls, the boy mimicked the gorilla and even started throwing things into the enclosure. I could never understand why some people enjoy teasing caged animals. I think it's cowardly and cruel. Apparently, the caretaker agreed with me. She had gone around through the caretakers' office behind the enclosure and appeared behind the group of offending kids.

"Stop teasing him, right now!"

Surprised, the boy fell back on a typical teen response.

"He started it."

I almost laughed. Was he actually blaming the gorilla?

"I saw you. You are scaring him. You need to leave."

The group turned to continue down the path.

"Not that way."

She pointed towards the entrance.

"That way. Leave Gorilla Land now!"

Heads down, they disappeared in the direction from which they came. I wanted to applaud the caretaker. Mostly people in the park were well behaved and seemed to enjoy the park.

The working conditions were pretty good, as costume shops go. Like most amusement parks, the pay was low, but not bad for the Tampa area. The hours were regular rotating shifts and only a little call for overtime. There were free tickets to the park every month, and a case of the parent company's finest was available each payday, as well. It was not a product I used, but there was always someone who was having a picnic or barbeque who welcomed extra beverages. None of the other companies I worked for had those kind of perks.

Unfortunately, I could see early on, there were going to be no opportunities to advance in this job. Since we all did our own pattern making and cutting, there were no step advances. Full time costume jobs were few and far between in Florida, that meant the manager and assistant manager would not be moving on any time soon. They did all the designs. That meant there was no opportunity to design either. It was time for me to move.

18 THE MINNESOTA NICE AND A CRISIS

I was back in Minnesota again; this time, cutting and sewing for an independent costume company that made walk around costumes for Sesame Street touring companies. I don't remember much about the costumes except that I made feet for Grover and a few other characters. There was a lot of fake fur and toxic glue involved and it was the first place I worked that had a proper fume room.

It was another one of those small close knit groups that squared off in clicks according to their weird personalities. There was the cutter from Lou'sianna, who hated the Neville Brothers. The snarky manager who would allow no Indigo Girls to be played on shop music system. Then there was the girl who was always late.

She'd come in ten or thirty minutes late most days. Rather than come in quietly, so as not to attract attention to her tardiness, she'd have new story each day.

"Do you wanna know why I was late today? I needed to get my coffee and bagel, but when I got to Trader Joe's it wasn't open, so I had to wait for them to open."

Most people in Minnesota are genuinely nice. But there is something called the Minnesota Nice. If you go to a gathering where you don't know anyone and they seem to be bending over backwards to be nice to you, watch out. They are just trying to get you to talk about yourself, so they can criticize you later. The saying goes that when you go to a party where you don't know anyone, you have to send a friend in as your point person to stay after you leave and tell you what they really thought of you.

I liked living in Minneapolis. It is a small city with lots of parks. They call Minnesota the land of ten thousand lakes and there truly are lakes everywhere. Minneapolis alone has thirteen lakes, all surrounded by public space. I was just three blocks away from a park with a small lake. I loved the way they had provided room for walkers, runners, skaters, and bikes. There are two lanes each way; one for walkers and runners and one for those on wheels. There are no signs, so I used the wrong lane the first couple times out. No one tried to stop me or give me a hard time. They just let me figure it out on my own. Quite a change from East Coast people who use every opportunity to tell you what to do.

There's also a long trail along the Mississippi River that goes across to St. Paul, where I saw a flasher. There aren't many places you can hide along the river trail, but perverts always seem to find a way. It was just around a curve with a few trees and a park bench in the center. There he was all relaxed with his private parts taking in the sun. They'll do anything to get attention.

When I was in high school, there was a man who would sit up in a tree naked and call out to people as they walked along underneath him. That one was a little more shocking. Nobody likes a snake in a tree.

***

Minneapolis and St. Paul are known as the twin cities because the only thing that separates them is The River. Both are very livable cities that haven't been overrun by high rise apartments. You can still live in a house in Minnesota. Minneapolis has a small downtown, which is more or less the cultural center. The night club where Prince started out was still there at that time. It has the Guthrie Theatre and the Walker Art Center. St. Paul is the intellectual center. It had more bookstores than any other city I've ever visited. Minneapolis is currently ahead of St. Paul on bookstore count. But St Paul definitely has the most concentration of bookstores, by neighborhood. You can go to a bookstore, then a coffee shop, another bookstore, and a coffee shop all afternoon. There's nothing like sitting in a funky coffee shop with a new used book on a rainy afternoon.

OK, it'd true Minneapolis' Mall of America is the largest shopping mall in

America. I didn't know that when I moved there; I usually avoid shopping malls. But I did go there just to see it. And yes, it does have a small amusement park in the center. It took an hour to walk around one level. That was enough; I had to leave after that. Stores in shopping malls are just not that different. Why would anyone want to spend an entire day at a shopping mall? How many kinds of trendy jeans and tee shirts can there be?

I spent just enough time in Minneapolis to get to know the Twin Cities area. I ran, I walked, I read books in coffee shops, I sketched in the Walker Museum. I liked it.

***

But when you're in theater, just when you get to like a place, it's time to go. I had one more Minnesota gig at a little theater in a small town called Lanesboro. It's always nice to drive out of the city into the green of the countryside. Minnesota is mostly flat with rich farmland, but as you go south and east it becomes gradually hillier with bluffs along the rivers as you get closer to the Wisconsin side. There's no sense of elevation in these Midwest states with no mountains. When the landscape changes, it's a surprise.

To get to Lanesboro, you take Highway 52 south from Minneapolis to Fountain and turn east on County Road 8. From here the landscape moves gradually downward until you are running along a bluff. The road winds down the bluff and at the bottom, just before you get to the Root River, there is Lanesboro.

It's a favorite weekend getaway for people from Minneapolis and Rochester. It's main street is filled with gift shops, bakeries, and restaurants; punctuated with a few bed and breakfast inns. Back then there was a German restaurant with an Oompah band that played every afternoon. There was a park where a local farmers' market appeared every weekend and a nice little library. Down at the end of the street was the Commonweal Theatre, Lanesboro's one and only live theater.

I was housed in a big old frame house where I shared upstairs rooms with several of the actors. There were bicycles in the garage that we could use on the Root River Rails to Trails Bike path that ran behind the house. It was my main work place, too. There was a big shop in the back with room for my craft work and a carpenter's shop besides. However I quickly realized I wouldn't be wanting to use the kitchen. The refrigerator hadn't been cleaned out in a long time; there wasn't even enough room for each person to store their own food. I got a part-time job at one of the local restaurants, in hopes of getting at least one nice meal each day. Of course, things didn't work out quite that way. I was told I could get a free meal there, but I wasn't allowed to eat until after we closed. Of course, the kitchen was closed, too, by the time I finished my own clean-up duties. They were nice people, though, who served excellent meals, and were a stand out over the more humble fare at most of the other restaurants. It was always busy and the tips were good. I stayed until dress rehearsals started, then gave my notice. I had a lot of work to do before the show went up. Besides, I was a lousy waitress; it stressed me out.

I had done costumes and masks for a the Commonweal's performance of Medea. It was a new theater at the time with a wonderful ensemble group of performers. It's still going strong today in a new theater space and has become a main attraction for locals and tourists alike in Lanesboro. This was one of those special experiences where things just go right. The management, crew, and actors all enjoyed each other's company and it resulted in a successful show all round.

By the last week, I was going in circles; prepping the costumes, taking interview calls for the next job, and then there was the call I never expected. I had not heard from my friend Ken in quite a while. We had been exchanging letters and e-mails, and having a phone call about once per month since I left Allentown. But I had not heard from him at all since I'd been in Minnesota. I know that friends generally fade away when you move around a lot. Usually I consider lack of communication one of the signs that I'm no longer a part of their lives. It usually means it's time to let go. But with Ken, it was different. We'd been close when I lived there and he had kept up regular contact with me until the last few weeks. He had traveled a lot himself and knew how important keeping those ties were, especially by phone. I had left several messages without a call back or an email. This was different. Something told me there was something wrong.

I decided to do something I never do. I called his office. I knew his administrative assistant and was confident she would be diplomatic, even if for some reason he just didn't want to talk to me. When she answered the phone and gave her my name, she remembered me right away; I'd done some sewing for her. I apologized for calling at work, but said it wasn't like him not to write or call and I was a little bit worried.

"Is everything alright?"

"Didn't you know? Ken is in the hospital. He's dying."

It literally hit me like a punch in the stomach. I let out an involuntary wail, bent over double, put my face on the desk and started crying uncontrollably. I could hear her on the other end of the line apologizing. She knew there was no gentle way to put it, but we always hope we can find that best way. I pulled myself together and picked up the phone. Was there anything I could do? Was there time to see him?

"No don't come. He won't know you. He has an inoperable tumor behind his left ear. He is totally deaf and blind. There's nothing you can do."

"At least it wasn't AIDS," I said naively.

But of course it was. I knew AIDS was an immune deficiency, but had never really thought about what that meant. It manifests itself in so many deadly ways. Today, many people are living for years with positive HIV without having full blown AIDS. There are new treatments and it is no longer an epidemic. Back then, it was devastating and the form it took was unpredictable.

I had lost my oldest and best friend to cancer while in college. Since then Ken had been the only person with whom I was really close. This was the beginning of learning to deal with loss. After the phone call, I couldn't think. I went out to the garage and got on a bicycle and headed out on the trail. I needed air, it was hard to breathe. It started at a solemn leisurely pace, but I found myself pedaling faster and faster. Tears came back and were streaming down my face. I kept pedaling and crying until I couldn't go anymore. The other people on the trail must have thought I was crazy, but I didn't care. Once I stopped I was spent. I went slowly back to the house. Tonight was dress rehearsal and I needed to shower and dress, and be back stage early.

I didn't want to talk about it, but I had to explain because the tears had been coming in waves all afternoon. When it hit me I couldn't control it. I just made a short announcement before we started, asking them not to stop or be surprised if I left the theater during the performance. They were kind and understanding. Hal and his wife Adrienne, the co-founders took me out for a delicious pancake breakfast the next morning and I left feeling sad but nurtured. Pancakes can do that.

19 THE SOUTHWEST ROUTE

This time I was not able to get a full season position. But I did get two back to back contracts at two different theaters in the San Diego area. Theater positions were becoming harder to find due funding cut backs. The NEA scandals over funding of art exhibitions by both Andres Serrano and Robert Maplethorpe had affected funding donations in all areas of the arts; and theaters, in particular were struggling. I was just hoping to make it through the next couple of years, with the idea that funding for the arts would recover and season contracts would again become available. It was a risk I took, in lieu of regretting not doing it down the road.

I left from Tampa, assuming the train would head northwest along the Gulf route and then continue on to New Orleans. What I didn't know was that there was no northwest rail line. It took eight hours to get out of Florida. The Sunset Limited line circled back to the east coast and the cars headed west were changed off in Jacksonville. It wasn't really an express train until it left Jacksonville.

Once we changed off and headed west things went pretty smoothly. We had a couple of hours rest stop in New Orleans. Enough time for lunch in the historic French Quarter and a walk around. It was a quiet afternoon, but it was quite pleasant to walk around without all the crowds. Not much happens here until after dark and we would be long gone before then.

My seatmate got off in Houston and I was hoping for an empty seat, which would allow me to stretch out a bit and sleep through the night. No such luck, a cheerful lady with a sweet Texas accent, who got on in Austin, was my travel companion until San Antonio. You just never know who you are going to meet when you travel. Some trips you can go the whole trip without speaking to anyone but gas station attendants, waitresses, or ticket sellers. This lady had lived here entire life in Texas and she had stories. I always like a story, so I was fascinated.

The train stopped less than ten minutes out of Austin. There was an emergency, someone was ill. We had to wait until an ambulance arrived from Austin before we could continue on our journey. This gave us time to get to know one another while we waited. Once we were on our way, she started pointing out pioneer sites to me as we moved along the Texas flatland. We chatted for a while and then decided to go to the observation car until dinner time. I still had my Olympus OM1 SLR camera with me. I miss that camera. Digital cameras have eliminated the need for film, but they have done nothing to enhance the quality of the photos. There's nothing like continuous color.

I was snapping pictures of all the little abandoned ranch houses and historic sites as I listened to some Texas history that I would never read in any books. I was planning to label the shots and add the stories to my journal when I got to San Diego. This was a once in a lifetime conversation. I was so excited to look at the photos once I got them processed. I ripped open the envelope and looked at the first one; an old shack of a ranch house with a few slats of the corral fence left with tumbleweed roundabout. The next one showed an old ranch house with the remains of an old barn and some tumbleweed. The third one, an old shack with tumbleweed and cactus in the front. Sadly, I had not had a way to record the stories.

We had dinner in the dining car; a well executed Tex-Mex menu to rival the more traditional meat and potatoes one I had experienced on The California Zephyr a couple of years earlier.

After my friend got off in San Antonio, I thought about all that history. We all have a history and when you know the stories of your family and even your neighbors, you have a sense of belonging. My family had stories, too. They were mostly legend, I'd have to write about them some other day.

The San Diego station was a well preserved early twentieth century building in the Spanish Colonial Revival style. It had a much more welcoming feel than some of the urban stations that looked more like warehouses than introductions to a city. The trunks were off loaded to the baggage area where I left them until I could find a suitable place to live. I arranged a room at the local YMCA for the first few days and had a taxi take me there with just the suitcases. It was walking distance to the theater and I figured I could put up with it for a few days.

I didn't really think about the fact that San Diego had a large naval base and the atmosphere might be a lot different than the Y on Manhattan's West Side. The male and female rooms were not on separate floors. The bathrooms were separate but didn't really feel safe, or clean. None of the guys bothered me, but I did see women wandering the halls in dressing gowns, going in and out of different rooms. That part I didn't mind so much.

The linens were clean and the bed wasn't too lumpy. But it was night time when I found out the real problem with this place. I saw some cockroaches, but didn't think much of it. I had lived in Hawaii and Florida, so I had was used to the fact that in warm climates they are always there. Generally, you only need to turn on a light before you step out of bed and they will scurry away. I was tired and glad to have a bed after the long journey. I fell asleep quickly, but it wasn't long before I woke up. Something was crawling on me. I turned on the light and saw a roach crawling across the bed spread. OK, so I would have to sleep with the lights on. That would discourage them. I drifted off again but awakened with a start, slapping at my face. How could this be? A roach with no fear? I jumped out of bed and shook out the bed clothes. I inspected the bed again and replaced the bed clothes carefully. I wouldn't be sleeping this night. Sitting up in bed with the lights on, it didn't take long to discover the worst of the problem. Roaches were crawling up the walls and across the ceiling. There were so many of them that they ran into each other. When that happened one of them would fall from the ceiling onto the bed.

I've never been so anxious to get out of a place in my life. I was relieved to find a note on the bulletin board at work from a lady who had a room for rent in the Mission Hill district the next morning. I didn't wait. I called her immediately and reserved the room, sight unseen. She offered to pick me up after work and I didn't hesitate to accept, although I was now embarrassed for her to know where I had been staying. I was waiting outside with the suitcases when she arrived and she took me around to the station to pick up the trunks.

She was a retired social worker, now in her eighties and one of the best drivers I've ever seen. Believe me I know drivers. I was a school bus driver in L.A. for seven years before I began this adventure. Her house was a nice little three bedroom on top of the hill above the city. There was one other roommate, another costumer who was making her living doing costumes for Celtic dancing teams. They were very popular then and there was always good money in team dance costumes because you got the order for the whole team.

The costumes have an interesting evolution in the United States. I'm not sure if Celtic dance became popular because of Riverdance or if it was the other way around. But at that time, June was doing a lot of costumes with ornate Celtic designs on the bodices and skirts. She told me, when she started out a few years before no one would dare to wear such bold costumes trimmed with intricate Celtic designs unless they were really top dancers. Now it had changed and most of the dance teams wanted fancy designed costumes. The top teams were now wearing very plain costumes. I always admired her for making her own business. At that time I would never have had the courage to even try doing production sewing on my own.

***

San Diego is a beautiful town. The weather is balmy all year round. It is friendly to walkers and bicyclists, there was a good bus system and a new light rail system. The San Diego Zoo, California's largest zoo; the San Diego Museum of Art; and the San Diego Museum of Natural History were a short walk from the theater within Balboa Park. In addition, there was a small arts district just beginning to grow in the Old Town area. It was my kind of town.

Of course, there were restaurants of every size, quality, and price range just down the hill from where I lived. Mexican food had become ubiquitous in California, even in the chain restaurants. They all had their taco plates; in San Diego the fish taco was the specialty in many restaurants. The secret is, if you want real Mexican food in California, you go where the Mexicans eat.

Of course, there were lots of little mom and pop restaurants, some of them were good and some a little questionable. Then how do you find good Mexican food in San Diego? Look for a takeout restaurant with a long line of Mexicans going out the door. There's a reason the line is long. It's kind of like that in Asia. One of my Taiwanese students once told me not to worry about long lines in Taiwan, "If there's no line, it's not good."

My first San Diego assignment was my second gig at a major Shakespearean theater and it was a good tech experience. Directors love to play around with the periods when doing Shakespeare; and that means plenty of new period costume work. There were fur muffs that could only be hand sewn, bustles and corsets to be made, and hats to be trimmed. I enjoyed the work, but it was for only one show. I was scheduled for two more shows at a local theater, but one was canceled due to funding issues. I would barely cover my expenses before the work in San Diego ran out.

I was assisting the shop manager at this second assignment and one of my coworkers from the Shakespeare company was stitching. I felt it was good experience, working with the shop manager, although it was mainly running errands. San Diego was small and did not have a lot of the things designers wanted, but Los Angeles. was a couple of hours away. It had everything a designer could want outside of New York. Luckily, I had lived in L.A. for seven years and knew my way around. Great, now I knew the costume shopping in New York and L.A.

When there was a production meeting or the designer was out of town, I often had down time. The crew manager was surprised when I came out of the office one day and asked if they needed help. What a question, there was always something else that needed doing in a costume shop. She looked quizzical and asked me what I could do. I told her, anything from stitching to pattern drafting although I enjoyed hand sewing. I figured that might be the best place for me. Since I might be called away at any moment, I couldn't be relied upon to do any big projects. She paused a moment and then handed me some detailed handwork to do. I gave a sigh of relief. "I thought I had done something taboo for a minute there."

"No," she said, "we're just not used to having an assistant who knows how to sew."

I thought about it and realized that the assistant position might be considered a job for a newly graduated design student. I was beginning to see a pattern here. In traditional business, it was best not to let anyone know you could type, if you were in management. Designers often didn't sew or at least pretended it was beneath them to do it. This was a glass ceiling, I was never able to break through.

There were lots of ups and downs and as one of my compatriots used to say,

"It's all part of the adventure."

The regional theater circuit is a small world and the longer you stay in it the more you run into the same people. Managers tend to stay put, but crew members generally travel around a lot, until they find a company that really suits them and then they stay. I had already run into an actor from my time in Minnesota when I was in grad school. I declined to talk about the scandal that happened while I was there, but he did inform me that the shop manager had been fired and I would have been the manager, if I'd stayed. I'm not so sure that would have been a good way to get promoted, and I really wasn't ready for it.

There was one other person from the Shakespeare company that moved with me to the second San Diego job. She was a stitcher and this time It was her turn to be ostracized. For some reason, the cutter for her team took a dislike to her and made a point to humiliate here at every opportunity. They had a wedding dress on their costume list and she decided that my friend should not be allowed to work on it. Instead of just giving her another assignment, she announced to the rest of her crew that her nemesis was not to be allowed to touch it. Once the gown was up on the mannequin, she would make this announcement every time she had to leave the room.

"I'll be back in a few minutes. Don't let HER touch it."

Why would she touch it if she wasn't working on it? Of course, now she did. As soon as, she-devil left the room, she would go over and touch it for no reason. Childish though it seems, this type of behavior goes on all too often in theater.

There was a tailor I'd met from Baltimore on the crew, as well. We took our lunch together in the park quite often and made a weekend trip to L.A. together. It was nice to be back and I was pleased to find I still remembered my way around the main streets after a ten years absence. We parted ways, but I heard he was working for an independent costume shop that did a lot of work for the circuses down in Florida. You never know where you will end up.

***

I had worked a season at Oregon Shakespeare Festival, during grad school and hoped to get on there after San Diego, but the season was half over and they were letting people go, not hiring. I had a lot of good memories from my first season, though.

Ashland is a small town in Southern Oregon. It was known for its quiet old fashioned charm and it's one thriving business was the Oregon Shakespeare Festival. Ashland has the best known Shakespeare festival on the West Coast. Comparable to Alabama Shakespeare Festival in Montgomery, it attracts audiences from all over the country. It was the only theater company I worked for with such a reputation and the whole town knew it, so living in Ashland as a Festival employee had its perks.

Oregon Shakespeare Festival brings thousands of people to Ashland every year who might otherwise by-pass it as a sleepy little town. The houses were mainly little white cottages with white picket fences. It was like walking through a story book scene of the ideal American town. There was one house I always remembered. It was a well kept little cottage, like most of the houses, but the front yard had been planted entirely with flowers. There was no lawn, just a riot of flowers. It reminded me of Emily Dickinson and all her poems on nature, especially flowers. I always wondered who was so bold to plant only flowers, but then I thought of Emily Dickinson, bold only on paper. Perhaps an aging gardener planned this scene to be able to watch from the window when she could no longer go out to garden. I passed that house each time on my way to the library. Like the little house, the library was another early twentieth century building. It had a small well kept collection and I was glad of that since traveling prevented me from having a personal library.

I was an avid reader and I made it a point to get a library card in every town I lived in. At one time I had quite a collection of them. In Ashland, there were no questions asked other than my address and my employer. Unlike my experience in Pennsylvania, they were not offended by my profession. They were happy to offer me use of their collection and welcomed me to the community. I walked back towards home along the little shopping street and stopped into the many craft and book stores. I made a few purchases and was given a discount in each store as an OSF employee. How nice to be treated with respect.

It was not always so. In one town where I worked for the local theater, they tried to refuse me a library card because of my association with the theater. They said they only gave library cards to permanent residents. I produced my driver's license and voter registration. Yet, the librarian was still not accommodating. There are times when you just have to make a scene to get what you want. I raised my voice enough for the other people in line to hear.

" I am a resident of this town, I have a full-time job, and I am a registered voter. You cannot refuse me a library card. It is one of the few public services I take advantage of and I intend to have it. If you don't give it to me, I will call my city counselor; perhaps then you will be a little more obliging."

I got the library card. The line moved on and I carried my selections home with my new library card safely stored in my wallet along with several others from my collection.

I do have to admit, there might have been some unreturned books at this particular library. Small theaters with struggling actors and crew tend to breed sticky fingers. At one theater, someone actually filtched my opening night gift from my favorite designer. I always thought that was a low trick.

Oregon Shakespeare Festival was different; employees were mainly happy, and actors were too well respected to cause trouble. At any rate, it was nice to be in a town where I was welcome.

20 VEGAS SHOW GIRL

I don't fit in well in conservative structured environments, and grad school was no exception. I had nothing in common with my professors and even less with other students, so I didn't make many new friends during that time. However, I did meet one kindred spirit. She was one of those women who are smart, yet so beautiful she stopped traffic, but that wasn't what we had in common.

What a combination! We were both disenchanted with our choice of higher education. The university overall was rated well, but that doesn't necessarily work out in reality. Only certain programs may be highly rated, and here, there was an atmosphere of hostility within the faculty in both our departments. We were paying for an education and being treated like the enemy. Even if you got into a good program, supporting yourself on a campus that is located in a job poor area made it a tough pill to swallow for adult students. Most of us were buried in debt.

Gilly was used to getting well paid and was shocked to find all the jobs in the university and the town were minimum wage. She was premed but opted out after the first year. University of Nevada, Las Vegas had a good premed program and she could easily find work that would pay her expenses.

I was getting ready to leave, too. I had completed the second year of my MFA program and had realized it wasn't going to be worth racking up more financial aid debt. No one in theater cared if you had a degree unless it was from one of a half dozen respected theater programs in the US that actually graduated actors and designers who got hired.

We stayed in touch and when I ended up in San Diego, Gilly was still in

Vegas. She showed up one Friday evening expecting to stay with me. She was the kind of person who was used to having things done for her. I was renting a room in a house with a retired lady and one other roommate. Since, I was new there, it was a little awkward asking to have a guest, but since it was only for the weekend, it would be ok. Besides, I had the best landlady in the world. She was always so nice and kind; I felt welcome there from day one.

You have to understand something about Gilly. She wasn't a bad person. She was very sweet, she just didn't know what it was like not to be treated like she was special. With her knockout looks and sweet personality, good things just seemed to fall in her lap. Consequently, she had a lot of good stories which were a lot more fun than mine.

Her family wasn't super rich, but they did have enough money to give her things I couldn't imagine, like a gap year trip to Europe. Like a lot of high school grads, she was traveling with a friend. They traveled through Paris and then down to the French Riviera, staying in hostels and budget hotels. For some reason, her friend decided to go home after one night in Nice. They checked out of their hotel and her friend left for the train and a flight home from Paris.

Gilly hadn't planned on this. She didn't want to go home. Their journey wasn't finished; besides which, her dad had divorced her mom the year before and had since gotten remarried. It wasn't possible to stay with him and his new young wife. But what to do?

She went down to the harbor and sat on her suitcase to think. She could at least enjoy the view and the beautiful sunset before deciding where to go next. After a few minutes, a man on one of the yachts noticed her sitting alone and called out to her.

"Would you like to come on board for a glass of champagne?"

"Why not," she thought. She'd nothing better to do.

This was nice. She had a comfortable seat on deck and a glass of champagne. She could worry about what to do later. She was a girl that lived in the present. Her gentleman friend excused himself after a few minutes, but she didn't think anything about it. Just as she was finishing her glass of champagne and thinking she ought to say her goodbyes and go, all of a sudden she hears a deep, "Phoot, phoot!" and the yacht starts pulling out of the harbor. Shanghaied!

Well, if one was going to be kidnapped, being stranded on a yacht in the Mediterranean with a good supply of champagne wasn't so bad. It turned out that the gentleman was actually the captain, not the host. The owners had ordered him to cast off and he wasn't going to explain that he had a woman on board. Better to wait until they were well underway, then they couldn't get rid of her until they arrived at their destination.

Gilly was introduced to the hosts and spent most of her time with them after that. There were no other guests, just the host and hostess, the captain and herself. They were both very gracious and treated her like an honored guest instead of an accidental stowaway. But Gilly knew the host was paying too much attention to her. Madame wasn't going to want her hanging around once the arrived in Pisa.

Gilly was given a small cabin near the captain, which kept her away from the host, but not from the captain. Cleverly planned, I'm sure. However, the lock on the door spoiled his plans. After making his best efforts to persuade her, he finally understood that nothing intimate was going to happen. They became good friends from then on.

They docked in the port at Pisa and the owners left for their villa. Gilly was left behind with the captain. He wouldn't be needed on the yacht. It was going into drydock for the winter. They wouldn't be going back to France until next season. Gilly could go with the captain to Florence where he would be caretaker for the winter in his employer's summer home. Everything they needed to live was provided and she and the captain had become comfortable with their friendship. He had other fish to fry and he wasn't going to continue wasting his time to persuade a young girl to do his bidding.

Gilly's parents weren't looking for her, since they had expected her to be gone for a year. It was still warm when they arrived, but within a few weeks, it started to get cold at night. By November it started to rain and it started to get cold in the daytime, too. Gilly had only brought summer clothes. She was from Florida and had not planned any trips to the mountains in winter. Captain's English wasn't very good and she had studied French, not Italian. But he understood when she hugged herself and said,

"Please, Cap, it's cold. I need a coat."

Without hesitation, he went to the downstairs hall closet and opened it. Inside was a whole collection of coats and winter accessories. They found a nice leather and fur trimmed coat that fit her perfectly. It would keep her warm all winter until they sailed back to the Riviera and she headed back home.

During the holidays, gift baskets started to arrive. Even though everyone should have known the owners weren't there in the winter, still they sent gifts. They were huge baskets with perfect beautiful fruit. Even one of these baskets had more fruit than the two of them could eat. So, Gilly took one of them to give to the homeless.

She was like that. In Las Vegas, she would buy a supply of sweaters from thrift stores and keep them in her car to give to the homeless people who so often stood on the median with their signs. Vegas is in the desert, but at nighttime in winter the temperature drops rapidly. She didn't have money to give them, but she'd roll down the window and yell,

"Hey, do you want a sweater?"

They were always happy to have something warm.

So, there was Gilly, wandering around the streets in Florence. There were no homeless people in her upscale neighborhood, but she only had to walk down hill into the town to find someone. The first poor old man she saw was so surprised when she gave him a huge basket of fruit, all wrapped up in cellophane and bows!

She said, "Boun Natale."

And he said, "Grazie mille," over and over.

There were no presents to give out in San Diego; just finding ways to entertain Gilly. I had to work a half day on Saturday with Gilly tagging along. I didn't have any errands to run that day; I was helping out with last minute finishing for the current show.

Gilly was bubbly and talkative, as usual, but the crew wasn't feeling chatty. There can be a lot of pressure the week before load in, so things can get pretty tense.

"You can stay and hangout, Gilly. But if you stay, you have to help."

She was sure she could find something to do on her own and she was gone in a minute. The crew were holding back the laughter until she left.

"That sure got rid of her quickly!" my friend Leah whispered.

We met up in the afternoon to go to the beach. Amazingly, Gilly had acquired a car. First she went to the beach near La Jolla Village to sun bathe. It wasn't long before someone came along and told her a family with small children was coming that way and wouldn't she please put on her top. Gilly was still used to the European way and was somewhat put off by this, but complied.

Shortly after that she donned her clothes and went for a stroll along the waterfront shops. Seeing a salon with no customers, she went in and asked for a haircut. With pouty lips and big sad eyes, she told him she was just a student and she couldn't afford the usual upscale price that the La Jolla ladies paid. She got the haircut and the loan of his car. They were having dinner later.

In the afternoon we went to Black's Beach, the open secret nude beach near La Jolla. This wasn't a public beach, it was accessed by a steep trail down a bluff. Perfect for nude sunbathing because it couldn't be seen from the road. Anyone who climbed down here knew what to expect. I had tendonitis in one ankle, so I put a tension band on that side. I gave the other one to Gilly to support her still weak, but newly mended, broken ankle.

We found a good spot, but within ten minutes were surrounded with guys. With a topless Gilly, it was bound to happen. I looked pretty good, too at that time, but Gilly—everyone wanted to talk to her. Oh well, I enjoyed the view. There was a Native American guy who stopped by to chat with dark hair down to his waist and the most perfect body I have ever seen. I mean everything was perfect! No harm in in enjoying the view, right?

The interesting thing about this beach was that everyone was so polite. It helped that there were two of us. Plus, a few families with kids were also enjoying the sun. There were a lot of people stopping to talk, so no one had a chance to make any moves. Besides, there was a kind of unwritten rule on nude beaches that it was for enjoying the sun, not for cruising. At that beach, at least, the rule was respected.

Of course, we got questioned about why we were wearing the tension bands on our ankles. Gilly very nonchalantly said,

"Oh, that's because we're both broken,"

Like we were a couple of dolls. That's Gilly.

Gilly went back to Vegas and finished premed without student loans. She had worked as a nude dancer until she broke her ankle. It paid well if you knew how to work it and she did.

I'd never been to a nude bar, but thanks to Gilly, I went once. Gilly's sister was working in a nude bar in Miami and she hadn't heard from her in a month. I was still in Florida at the time, so she asked me to go down and see if her sister was still working there. A friend from the Baltimore gig was visiting, so we went together.

When we got there, it was early. We thought, if she were there we might be able to talk to her before she had to start work. She wasn't; but we didn't know that until later. The manager told us two things. No females allowed without a male escort and they couldn't give out any information about any of the girls. So, even if she did work there, he wouldn't be able to tell us. I gave him the name and asked if he knew her to tell her to call her sister in Vegas. Say she was looking for her. That was all I could do.

While we were standing at the entrance, we could see the dance floor. There was just one couple in the whole place. Why would any guy bring a woman to a strip club? There was one stripper and all she did was stand there and unbutton a frumpy looking print dress. She didn't dance or make any effort to put on a show. It was the most boring thing I've ever seen. She was naked in less than three minutes.

There was more competition in Vegas, and Gilly was smarter than that. She had a white cut off fringed leather jacket she wore with white shorts and little boots. She'd shinny up the pole, hang upside down and let the jacket drop. That got their attention. She slid down and danced the rest of the act.

Needless to say, it was a popular act. She usually got top tips. One night she made so much money that when she turned in her commission for the night, the manager told her not to tell anybody because the girls would be jealous. But in general, she made her best money from regular customers. They were the ones that didn't want anything from her; they were just lonely men who wanted a pretty girl to talk to. Gilly could talk about just about any subject and listened well, so it worked for her. After her ankle healed, she didn't go back. She said, the money really helped, but it would be hard to go back. She didn't think she could do it a second time. That kind of a job only works if you don't have time to think about it too much.

I really liked Gilly, but she wasn't finding the right man and I couldn't help her in that department. The showing up unannounced and expecting to be pampered wore thin. She still had a kind heart, but I had other things to worry about. I felt sad to let that friendship go, but it was for the best. San Francisco was next and I had no idea how hard San Francisco was going to be.

21 SAN FRANCISCO

I had to say goodbye to San Diego. It had two really amazing theaters, each well respected nationally. But it takes more than two theaters to keep an on call costumer working. It could take years to get an offer for a full season job. Too bad I was so green when I landed that job in Allentown. I had no idea how hard it was going to be to get another long term assignment.

At least, I was working at bigger theaters now. But perks were all but eliminated. The National Endowment for the Arts was hitting theaters hard. I had been able to negotiate transportation and assistance finding accommodation in San Diego. However, the offer for the next job was a curt,

"If you can get yourself here, you have a job."

The San Francisco Opera has a huge budget for performers, directors, and musicians and designers. The costume and set budgets are large enough for elaborate costumes and sets and the large shop crews needed to put on these extravaganzas. Shop crew are just cogs in a wheel. It was a job, I took it.

***

The train looked like the best option again. The station was convenient and although there was no train station in San Francisco, AmTrak had a shuttle into the city from Emeryville. I found another women's hotel in the Lower Knob Hill area, which seemed good because it was walking distance to the costume shop.

At least this time, I was not threatened with eviction for my singular lack of personal connections. It was the only women's hotel in San Francisco and was more than a little more relaxed in its admission status than The Webster had been. Thus, some of my neighbors were not used to living on their own and their method of making friends involved accosting neighbors in the hallway as they attempted to make it to their rooms in a sprint with oversized bags of groceries before being discovered by the management, who frowned on food in resident's rooms. There was another one of those over stocked refrigerators on the first floor, along with a hot plate and a microwave. I didn't fancy putting my food next to something unidentifiable and covered with green fungus in said refrigerator. So, I made a note to search out all the cheap restaurants that appeared to be within the limits of the city health code.

On my first day of work, I had plotted out the shortest route to work. I took the nearest downhill street towards Market Street and heard screaming as I turned the corner. I had the good sense to stop until I identified the source of the disturbance. Good choice. A half a block away a rather large tattooed man was involved in a mostly nonverbal conflict with a scantily clad female. When a slap did not end the dispute, he backhanded her and she fell to the sidewalk. I stood frozen, watching as she attempted to get up and was kicked to the ground again.

"Stay down, stay down," I thought.

But my telepathic talents were apparently not getting through to her. As she tried to get up again, I decided a less direct route to work was in order.

As I became more familiar with San Francisco, I would learn that a one block detour was often necessary, as the city had no one particularly bad neighborhood, but random blocks which attracted unsavory residents. As a local you had to become familiar with these spots and their peculiar tendency to migrate slightly as one block became more run down and another received a facelift as gentrification edged in.

I arrived at the shop in plenty of time to do the requisite paperwork and join my assigned team. There were about six teams at a time and each was assigned a segment of the costume plan for each show build. Each team was lead by a pattern drafter and assisted by the cutter. Each had their own method. Some were meticulous, some were chatty, and some were a cut above the rest of us.

The head of my team was not a delegator. She carefully parceled out each costume to the six stitchers in pieces. She would often bring you a stack of rectangles and say, "Stitch two of each of these on this line." You cannot imagine how disconcerting this can be. Even factory workers get to know if it's their job to stitch one hundred sleeves that day or put in seventy-five zippers. I was used to being assigned an entire costume, even a whole ensemble start to finish. But I quickly learned to keep my mouth shut and just sew.

We each had our own sewing machine, but there wasn't an overlock machine for each team. So, whenever we had to overlock something, we had to go over to another team's work station and use theirs, when it was available. My friend from San Diego was on the other team and we would often chat a bit as we continued to sew. One day, I was pulled aside and told not to distract the other team members when I was using their machine.

Of course, the next time I went over there, my friend tried to start a conversation.

"Good morning."

I nodded.

"How are you?"

An attempt to smile while continuing to sew.

"Want to meet up after work?"

A look.

"What's wrong, why won't you talk to me."

Finger to lips and a whispered, "Later."

I hurried off back to my own work area. Talk about passive aggressive. Someone could have just said, "We prefer that you don't talk while you work." That's the only costume shop I ever worked at that did not allow talking.

Another way they would punish you was to send you to use the industrial mangle. They had one of those in a back room. It had a base large enough to steam iron a full width of fabric, which was necessary in order to preshrink fabrics that could not be washed. Actresses were famous for complaining about their costumes shrinking when it was actually the actress who was growing. Preshrinking eliminated a lot of unnecessary letting out of seams, not to mention, costumes hold their shape better if the fabric doesn't start shrinking after it's assembled.

The ironing was usually done by a laundry crew, but they kept strict hours, which meant sometimes we had to do it. I actually liked learning to use all the different machines, so, I only got to do this once. At least it was at the close of the evening, when there was no rush, unlike at the big shop in San Diego where the manager asked me to quickly steam ten yards of fabric with a small hand steam iron. They were in a hurry to have it for some reason. Every five minutes, she kept admonishing me to go faster. Until finally, I had to say, "There is a limit to how fast I can do this and still say I actually ironed it."

No response.

A few minutes later, she said, "You can stop now, they don't need it anymore."

You never know what weird task you are going to be asked to do and it's better if you don't know the reason.

The Opera was a bit militant, but I could see there were opportunities there. There was one crew that consisted of all Chinese tailors. Most shops just purchased men's suits retail or found a bespoke shop that could customize them quickly. But this shop made all the costumes for the major players. They were the singers on world tour and were to be pampered. Thus, the tailoring crew. One day, I made bold and asked the shop manager if I might be assigned to that crew. I'd had some tailoring training and I was keen to learn more. One of the visiting designers in New York had told us how they had brought in a retired Hong Kong tailor from San Francisco to do the period suits for *The Joy Luck Club* Her description of the resulting work was that "the seams were just kissed together." There were no press lines, the suits hung like they just appeared whole one day. I wanted to learn how that was done.

"No," she said, "Those tailors have all been working together for a long time. They don't train anybody."

Again, I had been naïve.

Tailoring was a lifetime profession. It wasn't something you did now and then. I had made several men's suits, but I was no expert and never would be. It's probably for the best. Tailoring is all about the details. It's fractions of an inch adjustments to create the illusion of the perfect male body. There's little room for creativity. I would have wanted more room to experiment. I was the girl whose mother would exclaim,

"Why can't you just follow the directions?"

"Because, I don't want to." I would think.

Even today, I don't get along with directions. I mostly knit because of lack of space. But I don't finish a sweater very often, because I spend more time figuring out all the changes I'm going to make, rather than following the directions. I think the most valuable thing I learned from costume training was how to visualize the structure of what I want to create. A lot of designers don't even sew, much less draft patterns. This can lead to costumes that don't look like what they imagined. A sketch can only show so much. If a pattern maker asks how you want something done, it's best if you can tell them. If you say, "Do what you think best," you have to be able to live with the result.

There was a lot of amazing talent in that costume shop. The best stitcher on our crew was a Hong Kong trained seamstress who'd been working at the Opera for more than ten years. She was the only one who ever gave me a compliment on my sewing skill and it meant more to me than it would have coming from just about anyone else. She had my undying respect. One evening before a dress rehearsal, three of us had volunteered to stay late in the shop to finish some of the hand sewing. There was Mary, Mark, and myself. As we were putting the finishing touches on some of the costumes that needed handwork; all she said was, "Your handwork is very good."

It made me proud. This was someone who had worked in shops where everything was hand sewn start to finish. She knew the final handwork was important. It was usually the only sewing that was visible on the outside of a garment. Like the brush strokes on a painting, hand sewing shows skill. A multitude of small machine sewing errors can be hidden on the inside of a garment, but the hand sewing is the piece de resistance.

***

The contract with the Opera shop ended for most of us when the last show of the season was up. There were costumes to be made for the ballet season which follows the opera; but that was an elite crew of mainly Russian women. The saying goes: "You have to belong to a secret society in order to make tutus."

Some people signed on for the next season. I was given my choice and I chose not to come back. I could see that I had gone as far as I could go with this experiment. The design jobs were few and far between and even the costume team leaders at this level came from backgrounds that did not include me. Everyone except the stitchers came from the top design schools and most of them were bilingual in French or Italian.

I wasn't going back on the road again. It had become financially unviable. I liked San Francisco and I wanted to stay for a while. It was an adventure just living here. But that's not the end of my road trips. It's just a rest stop, where there are different stories, and different people.

22 WHEELS

After I left the opera costume shop, I decided not to sew for other people any more. I had lost the pleasure of making things for myself and wanted to get that back. I secretly still hoped to become a costume designer, if only on a small scale. There were some opportunities in San Francisco, but the logistics of being a costumer in the San Francisco Bay Area without a car made it difficult to manage. I often spent more on transportation than I made, if I made anything at all.

Design wasn't going to be a way to make a living. I ended up working in the financial district during the height of an investment boom, just before the first big crash in the 1990s. Online investment was in its infancy, yet it had taken off like a rocket. And like a rocket, it was a disaster when it crashed. I had just passed my Series 7 broker's test when, the following day, I heard a wave of groans run through the cubicles on our sales floor. I turned to my computer to see the entire screen in red! It was the first time all the bids on Wall Street were computerized and when the first big sell off came, floor brokers couldn't pull their customers out of it fast enough to save them. Clients lost millions.

I knew my entry level status would make my tenure in this industry short lived, especially now. With that in mind, I paid off bills, started a savings account, and for the first time in years was able to afford small luxuries. I bought a bike and made several trips out of town with a friend for long rides in the hills. BART, (Bay Area Rapid Transit) was allowing bikes for the first time and my geographic reach was expanded significantly.

I had already been doing inline skates along the Embarcadero in the mornings and in Golden Gate Park on Sunday afternoons. I could roll slowly down Market Street to the Embarcadero and skate as far as

Fisherman's Wharf and the Marina, but there was a steep hill at the end of Van Ness Street just past the Dolphin Club, which was unskateable. My only option was to turn north and skate around Fort Mason, coming around past the Palace of Fine Arts and ending at Crissy Field. It was a long skate, but one I enjoyed on early mornings. It was usually too crowded for skating through the tourist area on the way back. Without too much trouble, a backpack with street shoes allowed me to bus back downtown.

All my other skates involved taking public transportation to a place where I knew there was a long stretch of paved sidewalk or a road with light traffic. Now the bike changed my life style. I could get to any place in the city in less than an hour. I had saddlebags and a rack on the back which allowed me to make a quick trip to Trader Joe's, a grocery store that was only six blocks away, but very inconvenient by bus. With the bike, I could take the saddle bags into the store with me and pack half the groceries in there. Sometimes I brought a backpack, too. I often had the saddle bags loaded up, a backpack on my back and another bag on each side of the handlebars. Shopping had never been so convenient. By bike, it was less than ten minutes. I could complete the whole trip in less than an hour, if I went when there were no long lines. It was the first good bike I'd ever owned and I rode it almost every day until I left San Francisco.

My life had more adventures in San Francisco, but less career success. Still, it was never dull. After the stock market crash, I spent an entire year doing temp work, where I meet more people and did more strange jobs than in any other time of my life. The travelling stopped for seven years. Because of all the strange experiences, I never thought about traveling again until it became so expensive I couldn't live there anymore.

23 THE MAN AT THE END OF THE PLATFORM

I always walked the platform when there was a long wait at a BART station. One day at the Richmond station I met a man standing on the front end of the platform in the sun. He was wearing the most unusual sunglasses I had ever seen. They were made of braided coils of silver wires wound together, curved and clamped just in the right places to fit perfectly. I commented on them and we began to chat. He had been a costumer in Los Angeles and had come back to the Bay Area after his health failed. Michael had one of those personalities that just seemed to attract people to him.

We had an hour to get acquainted before we reached San Francisco and by that time we were fast friends. He became my closest friend in San Francisco. We went to jazz concerts together at Yoshi's in Oakland, went for cocktails on the Beach Chalet on the west end of Golden Gate Park, and just generally had fun in the city. I was working in an art gallery near the Hyde Street cable car turn-around and sometimes he would just show up to take me to lunch. He was there on the phone when my crazy neighbors in my slightly slummy apartment were harassing me and there to celebrate when I had a big sale at the gallery.

The one thing he would not do was help me land a costume job in LA. He'd worked on all kinds of movies for more than ten years. He loved his job, but lived in constant fear of missing the next assignment. The competition was so fierce that when he was on the point of physical exhaustion, his friends had to make him take a vacation. Location shoots start before dawn for the crew and don't end until they lose the light. They often follow the daylight location shots with night shoots and if they are working on a studio lot, there is no limit to the number of hours shooting can continue. Costumers have to be there as long as the actors are there.

Designers come in only for a few days once shooting starts, but the costume crew stays to the bitter end. Fifteen hour days are typical and cocaine is included in the budget on the set with a lot of directors. It's a way to keep those crews going. I insisted that that wouldn't happen to me. I had been around drugs and drug users since my late teens and survived. I wasn't going to start using now in my forties.

The voice of experience prevailed. No one can stand up to those hours indefinitely. In theater, you have long hours the week before first dress and are back on a regular schedule working on the next show once the current one opens. Michael had ruined his health from using, at first just to keep up the pace of the shoot schedules, and later from addiction. He was the nicest person in the world and you would never have guessed he was an addict. He contracted hepatitis B and eventually psoriasis of the liver. By the time I met him he was going for regular treatments at USF Medical Center but was not recommended for a liver transplant. I never understood why he couldn't get on the list; I only knew he had argued bitterly with his physician about it. It only came up once; after that I knew he was beyond help.

Eventually, the treatments no longer worked and he didn't come into the city any more. The edema that comes with the advancing liver failure made it impossible for him to have any quality of life. The last time I talked to him was on the phone, he was very despondent, but was clinging to one last hope for a cure at a clinic in Mexico. I was so worried, he promised he would stay in touch. I had lost Ken and now when I had finally found another close friend, someone that I could tell anything and share my deepest feelings with, I was losing him. I never heard from him again. A couple of weeks later, a got a call from an American couple in Mexico. Michael had arranged to stay with them while he was being treated at the clinic. He never got any treatments. He had died in his sleep one night before he had even completed screening. He'd left my number with them as one of the people to call. They had a memorial service for him down there, but there was no way I could make it down there.

The crying started again. You think you will learn to bear up better, but there is no getting used to losing someone you truly love. That hole in my heart was getting bigger. I had heard other people use that expression, but until I lost Ken, and then Michael, I didn't know what it meant. There is just no other way to express it. It's a psychic pain. You feel like something has been ripped out of you leaving a big hole in your life that never heals.

The family funeral was the following week and I took the BART out to Richmond. His family sent someone to pick me up and they brought me to their house until time to go to church. I met his mother who was like an older sweeter version of Michael. The couple who drove me to the church had known Michael's family all his life.

"His grandmother is an even more beautiful spirit. When you meet here, you feel like you have met an angel."

I was so thankful Michael had a wonderful family life to support him.

There were pictures in the lobby from many of the films Michael had worked on, along with family photographs. He'd been cremated, so there was no coffin; just a memorial service. The minister kept his invocation short then turned the service over to the mourners to share their memories of Michael. His mother spoke first, then one by one friends stood up and told what a good friend Michael had been. The tears started again as soon as his mother began to speak. There was no sad talk about his illness, just happy memories. The weeping was for our own loss. There are so few people who have such a beautiful spirit. The couple I was sitting with were both crying, too We didn't stop crying until we were back in the car.

"I didn't think I had any tears left." the husband said.

It was exactly how I felt. I knew this time not to try to stop the crying. I thought I had cried enough to dry up all my tears, at least for a while, but the pain of loss was still there. I've lived on and travelled thousands of miles. I've left my own country behind. I've made new friends in many places, but true friendship is precious. It's not about how long you have known a person, but the rare deep bond that only occasionally occurs. Nowadays, few people value friendship, and few people merit it. But I wonder, at the end of their lives, what they will think it all meant if there were no friends that were worth taking the time to know intimately.

24 GREEN CARD

I had made a habit of attending Glide Memorial Methodist Church which sat on the border between Union Square and the Tenderloin. It attracted a congregation from diverse lifestyles and backgrounds from the poorest of poor who lived in the Tenderloin District, to middle class yuppie types who lived just up the hill bordering on the ritzy Knob Hill neighborhood, to tourists from countries around the world.

At first they there were no adult bible study classes, but when they hired a new assistant minister, bible classes were offered once a week. I attended those on a regular basis, too, for a while. Our class was invited to the minister's sixtieth birthday party and I went, hoping to get to know some of my classmates better and maybe meet some of the other church members. Glide didn't have the social groups that many churches had. They were in a high needs area, so most of their money went to supporting the needs of the community. They operated a free meal program, emergency housing, free counseling, and eventually built transitional housing for women with children. They did a lot of good for the community. But opportunities to get to know other members of the congregation were few unless you were in a recovery program or in the choir.

I loved our minister, so I was pleased to be invited to his birthday party. But I was also looking forward to the opportunity to socialize. I said hello to a couple of people from the bible class but I mostly recognized members of the choir. They were an important part of every church service. They had some amazing soloists, an outstanding music director, and a regular backup band. The music was incomparable! They rocked the house with gospel music every Sunday.

I eventually fell into conversation with a well dressed man from Tunisia.

He had entered the US by way of Canada and had made his way there as an entrepreneur, a term that was little used at that time. He asked me out for the following weekend and we went to a jazz club on upper Market Street. He talked about his country, his French mother, and his loss when both parents died. I talked about my work in the theater and how it had brought me to San Francisco. I still remembered my college French and he spoke to me in French when things started to get romantic. We had a second date at an Indian restaurant and by that time I was smitten. When I told a coworker at the shop, whom I'd known since San Diego, she said,

" He wants a green card."

"Oh, come on. Don't jump to conclusions. That kind of stuff only happens in movies."

I was wrong. There were tell-tale signs by the third date. During a conversation about interesting places in San Francisco, he mentioned that all the rich San Francisco ladies lunched at The Mark. Why did he know that?

He did come to America with money, but it had mostly run out when he got to San Francisco. He was working in a sandwich shop in Oakland, owned by Arab Christians. They had been very kind to him and he was impressed by how polite they were. But he wasn't sure they were going to keep him. Another red flag.

By the end of the evening he was telling me I had to start looking for an apartment. He didn't ask me, he told me. And by the way, I had to stop this "sueing," as he called my job at the Opera. It was clear why he had not been successful with the ladies who lunch.

It was clear that this was not going to work out, but he begged me not to drop him. I agreed to give him one more chance. It was my birthday the following weekend; we'd see how that went.

We were supposed to go out dancing. He took me to a restaurant, that I knew he could barely afford. After the meal, he made no attempt to leave. He ordered another cup of coffee, leaned back in his chair at our sidewalk table, and took out an expensive cigar. When he lit up I asked when he planned on heading out to the club. He replied that he had no more money, but we could go if I paid. I was pretty sure that would only result in him trawling the eligible women for someone with more money. I suggested we should go our separate ways. He knew I wasn't going to get my neck in that noose.

I wasn't going to waste this evening; I was going to have a good time on my own. As I crossed Market Street and headed off in the opposite direction, I heard him call out.

"You can call me if you want."

Fat chance.

***

The trumpet solo

There was a local jazz club a few blocks away and I headed that way. I always felt better when listening to some good live music. The band was good and the trumpet player came over to talk to me during the break. He seemed like a pretty nice guy, but I told him I was just there for the music. I love live jazz and there were few places in San Francisco where you could listen to good music for the price of drink. That night TJ came off the stage during his trumpet solo making his way through the small room. He stopped right in front of me, then turned leaned in with the trumpet turned away from my face; he and the trumpet were in profile just over my shoulder. I don't remember the song. I only remember the soft warm tones of the trumpet and every woman in that place envying me. This was hard to resist. He did ask me out eventually, but mostly he just wanted me to come and hang out during his gigs. I'd been out with musicians before and this didn't bode well.

I wasn't attracting the right type of man, I knew that, but I didn't know how to change it. At least I recognized it now. That was the last time I dated.

Part 2 - San Francisco Homelessness

25 THE LADY IN THE CHANEL SUIT

San Francisco was the end of my road trips. There would be more travel, but mostly by air. I stayed there for seven years trying to make it; wondering what direction to go next with my life. After the first year, I gave up on theater. It was a big disappointment. I had tried and failed and being able to say I tried didn't seem like much consolation. I had no backup plan. I had always told myself that I would be no worse off after my education than before. At least, they cannot repossess your education, you have that. I didn't know what a hard place San Francisco was going to be.

Yet this city was an experience in itself. It was charming, quaint, hip, and the place to be for young techies. It could also be tough, evil, and unforgiving. For the first time in my life, I lived in fear of being homeless. The homeless in San Francisco's downtown were very visible and you soon learned that you could be just one step away from homeless and not really know it.

I would often head down to the Embarcadero early in the morning; either running, blading, or biking. It was the one time of day you could get in some serious exercise without having to choose between being dodging cars or weaving in and out of crowds of tourists. Just after dawn was also the time when the homeless people were coming out of wherever they had found to hide and moving around to get warm.

The changes between neighborhoods in San Francisco were dramatic. Sixth and Market, just around the corner from where I lived was known as Crack Alley. Just one block away, on Fifth and Market, was the most posh new shopping center in San Francisco. In the early morning, there would often be someone standing on that corner outside the closed shops.

One morning, as I approached Fifth and Market, I saw a well dressed woman standing there alone. She was in a suit that looked like it could be a Chanel, she was in heels and her silver hair was done in an updo. As I got closer, I could tell there was something wrong with the picture. The suit didn't have that perfect pressed look from the dry cleaners, like it should. As I got closer, I could see the hair wasn't just right either. It looked like it had been slept in. She was shouting out her story to nobody. She told how she had gotten divorced and lost her health insurance and her house.

"You think everything is alright," she said, "but everything can be taken away over night."

I imagined a woman like her wouldn't even know where to go for help. As I passed her, I looked at her face. The makeup was all crooked and she had that crazed look in her eyes which I had seen so often on homeless people who were either in advanced stages of drug or alcohol addiction, or just had a mental break down. She didn't see me. She didn't even know I was there. She was calling out in desperation, but she couldn't see the people who were right in front of her.

26 STRANGE NEIGHBORS

At least I had a place to stay. My priorities were safe, clean, and quiet. My place was cheap; it had no windows, but it was a clean newly remodeled newer building. There was a combination lock on the door, so if you were careful, it was safe once you got inside. At least that was sometimes true. At first, I made an effort to be friendly to my neighbors. They all came from different circumstances, but they had ended up here while trying to get to a better place.

My next door neighbor was a man in his early thirties who was waiting tables. He'd been raised in the south and came to San Francisco to get away from racism. He was intelligent with an incredible vocabulary. He was in love with words. He could have been a great writer, but like so many people in San Francisco, he had a problem. He was an alcoholic and later became addicted to cocaine. At first he was very friendly and I often shared meals with him and the neighbor across the hall. But after a while, he began staying up late and talking loud. At first I would just knock on his door and ask him to keep it down. Sometimes he had company, but more often than not the argument I'd been hearing was with himself. Eventually the rantings became personal. I could hear him calling my name and shouting threats through the wall.

One particular evening he kept calling my name and saying "Where are you? Where are you?" Followed by "That's what's going to happen to you."

Unbeknownst to me, he was quoting from a murder scene in a David Lynch film. I happened to chose to see that film one afternoon on my day off. I sat straight up and froze in my seat in the half empty theater when the scene came on. It was a bloody scene in a bedroom with a woman who had apparently been hacked to death with a hatchet. Now, I was more scared going in the apartment than out.

I reported the problems to the owner and manager, and called the police a couple of times. The threats just got worse. One night he knocked on my door, I looked out the peep hole and recognized him. Just then my phone rang. It was my neighbor across the hall.

"Don't open the door. He's standing there with a board in his hands."

I wasn't about to open the door. This time the police did come when I called and things got quiet over there after that.

It takes ninety days for an eviction to take effect, so even though he was behind in his rent, I had two more months of living in fear. There were no more rantings, but I would hear him going in and out several times in the middle of the night. Everything was closed. I knew there was only one place he could be going and be back in less than fifteen minutes. It was the alley behind the building. The high from a of hit of cocaine can be as short as ten minutes once you're hooked, and he was really hooked.

About two weeks before he was due to be evicted, I started hearing strange noises at night. At first I thought it was a rat. The building was clean, but I had seen the rats in the street late at night. I would only take one getting in for it to take up residence. I would begin moving things to search for a hole and it would stop. I would go back to bed and it would start up again. When the apartment next door was vacated, the noise stopped. In a couple of days the crew came in to paint the apartment. One of the guys stopped to ask me if I knew anything about the last tenant.

"Only that he was crazy,"

I wasn't going to go into that story.

"Well," he said, " We noticed some holes in the wall and there was a smell. When we opened it up there were pieces of salami, bread, and all kinds of garbage. We had to clean it all out and replace all the dry wall."

It was the wall between his apartment and mine.

27 EX-CONS

Several of the tenants in my building were struggling artists and there was always some event afoot. I was invited to display my mask work in a show in a nearby café which had been organized by my neighbor down the hall.

On meeting Eli, you knew right away that there was something strange about him. He was a big man with wild grey hair and a walk that resembled someone jumping stepping stones over a brook while on a hallucinogenic drug. He did work hard, though. His one room apartment was covered floor to ceiling with paintings. He would work non-stop for a week and then pass out and sleep for two days.

He had a friend who lived in The Mission district, who would come by every day to check on him. Someone had to be sure he was on his meds and that they were working properly.

Vince was a Puerto Rican guy from the Brooklyn. He was the one person who enabled Eli to live on his own. Having met in prison, they watched out for each other. They were the ones you might have thought were dangerous, if you knew their background. But they were, also, the ones who brought tenants together.

On Thanksgiving, they were the ones who put out a spread for the six of us on the mezzanine floor and all our friends. How they found a turkey big enough for all of us and got it cooked, I don't know. Vince had a kitchen at his big Victorian house in The Castro, somehow, I doubt the turkey came from that oven. More likely, they acquired it from one of the local soup kitchens. Those places often had extra food, which they sent home with the volunteers at the end of the shift.

San Francisco had an abundance of free food, but distribution was not always well organized. Sometimes they would get a big donation and just hand things out; other times they barely had enough for everyone in the long lines that stood outside. St Anthony's in the Tenderloin once gave canned food out to the homeless. How they thought that would work, I don't know. Most of them didn't even have a can opener, much less a way to cook.

Up in our Market Street lofts, our Thanksgiving meal was a resplendent. Each of us found a way to contribute something. Some people had hot plates, others a microwave, or a crock pot. You would be surprised what you can cook up with a toaster oven!

This is how I found out, it wasn't the junkies that were going to be a problem. They were streetwise and protective and would go out of their way to help a friend. As it later turned out, I was lucky to be considered a friend.

Louis, the procurer of the carnivorous portion, had been a wall street stockbroker until he burned out on cocaine. He'd dropped out, left a wife and kids, and come to San Francisco, where his drug of choice was now heroin. He would regale me with stories of wall street and upper west side Manhattan social life. He had married into one of the moneyed families. However, his wife's family didn't like her attachment to a lowly stock broker who only made hundred thou' a year. They were happy at first, but their were signs that the gap in their social class might be more of a challenge than he had imagined. The night they gave their first dinner party the lights went out during the meal. No fuses were blown and after checking that the lights were not out in any of the other apartments; it occurred to him to ask her if she had called the electric company to have the lights turned on in their name.

"Aren't they always on?"

This was when he realized, her family's money put them in the class that had "people" to do things for them. She had no idea how things worked.

The family expectations and the pressure of Wall Street eventually got to him and he ended up on San Francisco with nothing but a cold curb on and drug habit to keep him company. He was off the street now, sharing an apartment with a friend, and like the rest of us living on the edge.

For a while, these three guys were my only friends and they did help to keep me sane while I adjusted to living in my windowless room in a city of glittering wealth. The city outside eventually became my refuge. But for a short while, these few friends helped me survive.

Eli and I would talk in the hall and he would occasionally do small favors for me. He fixed my coffee pot for me when I foolishly tried to use it to make hot chocolate. He finished hanging my masks at the show for me, when I had to rush off to work in the gallery. I couldn't help him with much, but I would mend the occasional garment. I, also, helped him learn to use a sewing machine when he acquired one. I was careful to keep a certain distance between us, never allowing anything more than friends.

However, once in a while I would visit in his apartment with one of the other neighbors. One night when a few of us were sitting around talking, Eli told us he had discovered there were some homeless teenagers living in the space above our floor. The idea seemed plausible, since it was scheduled to be remodeled for new lofts, but was currently not in use. He did janitorial work for the building and he said he had heard them on several occasions in his apartment and in the hallways.

He, of course, had sympathy for anyone who was homeless. He didn't want to out them, but winter was coming and he was afraid they might start a fire to keep warm. He was in a turmoil about what to do. He was also showing signs of paranoia. He had covered the air vent, which was the only way to get fresh air from outside, because he said he thought they sometimes watched him from there. The vent was on the wall near the top of the nine foot ceiling and it wasn't well light, but we could see there was a spot right in the center. He moved closer,

"Look, they've punched a small hole from inside. That proves it!"

He made a sudden gesture pointing towards it from up close—and a fly flew off the paper. We all went into hysterics! That was how I found out Eli was not only and ex-con and a junkie, but was also bipolar.

Still, he seemed harmless enough, despite some other habits, that didn't suit my lifestyle. In particular, he was into sadomasochism. Like a lot of people who are just over the line of deviant behavior, he insisted that he never tried to influence anyone else to come over to the dark side. It did have its dangers and those who shared its temptations revealed themselves soon enough. It's always a red flag when someone has to explain their weakness.

Eli and Vince had started a leather business to try to earn extra money. Vince had a young college student rooming with him and we had become friends. One evening Eli and I were both headed over to Vince's place and headed out together since we happened to be leaving at the same time. Eli was trying out a new leather piece he and Vince had designed. Not surprisingly, it was a leather choker, studded, with a detachable leash. I made no comment.

We were walking along just like two normal friends, when he asked,

"Would you like to walk me on the leash?"

Remembering his past assurance that he didn't push anybody to share his idiosyncrasies, I replied,

"No, it's really not my thing."

And all the while thinking,

"If it were, I certainly wouldn't be displaying it while walking down Market Street."

We took the F Market trolley the rest of the way up to the Castro, walking the two blocks to Vince's. Nothing more was said about the doggie incident. Although, Eli had gotten into a discussion with a teenager on the trolley about how useful this little trinket was, letting her know there were other things for sale, if she was interested.

Vince and Eli worked on their leather collection and Amy and I chatted. She had been a freshman at Humbolt State who had come up on a weekend trip with friends, staying behind when her friends left. She'd been living on the street when Vince had rescued her. That was one of the strange things about these guys, for all their strange habits, there was this protective side to them. They had seen it all, and they would go out of their way to rescue someone who was getting caught up in street life, before they couldn't get out.

Once they were finished with the leather work, Eli was ready to go home. I wanted to talk to Vince, so said I would come along later. I stayed for about an hour more then took the last trolley back down Market Street. It was a week night and quiet, but Vince and Amy walked me to the trolley stop. They knew, the time you are most likely to get harassed, robbed or assaulted was anytime you were standing around alone late at night. San Francisco is fairly safe, but I had walked home many a night to avoid standing and waiting alone at a bus or trolley stop.

When I arrived on my floor, I went quietly in the hall so as not to wake anyone. I turned the key slowly and opened the door. Something, fell on my head! As it slid to the floor, I saw it was a note. I opened it and it said,

"YOU F****ING BITCH! YOU ARE JUST LIKE THE REST OF THEM. I HATE YOU. ELI"

I was beside myself. I had to keep living on this floor and I certainly didn't want to see the angry side of Eli. My neighbor was still up and moving around. So, I knocked on his door and showed him the note. He laughed.

I called Vince and read the note.

"I don't know what to do."

He did not laugh. He was at my door in ten minutes. I described the walk and the leash. He wasn't surprised. But I had no idea that this would be seen as a rejection. Vince talked to Eli and he agreed not to bother me. But he sold the sewing machine because, he told Vince,

"It reminds me of that bitch."

So, much for avoiding the dark side.

28 SNUFF

Amy had come up to San Francisco with friends from Eureka on a weekend and had stayed on when her friends returned. Vince had taken her off the street and she'd been staying with him ever since. It was a strange arrangement. They were neither friends nor lovers. She had no money, so she wasn't officially a roommate either. She still hung out with some of her street friends and would sometimes be gone for a few days. Vince, would also be out of town for a few days when the company called him back to New York. Since the house was owned by the company, Amy had no key. She was left on her own on these occasions. There was never any formal arrangement between them and I think Vince figured she would grow tired of hanging out and go back to Humbolt eventually.

I ran into Amy early one evening on one of her lost weekends. It was getting dark and I asked her if she wanted to come up to my place to call Vince.

"No, I'm on my own for a few days"

She would be hanging out with friends later. I told her she could hang out at my place for a while and even spend the night if she wanted.

I didn't have a proper kitchen, but I had a small hotel refrigerator and a coffee maker. So, we had coffee and made do with something from the frig. I asked why she wasn't staying at Vince's. There had been an official roommate once, another company man, who watched the place. But things hadn't worked out and he'd been called back to New York for other duties. Since then, no one else had been allowed to live in the house. So, Amy's status was unofficial.

Amy and her companions would often get together on these leaves and pool their money for a cheap hotel and party. It wasn't nice but it got them off the street and they found ways to stay entertained until check out time the next day. One or two of them would go in and rent the room, then the rest of them would go up as visitors in ones and twos. It usually took a half dozen of them to come up with enough money for the room. So, they all just hung out and got high until it was warm enough in the morning to go back out on the street.

Little by little, more of Amy's story came out as we talked and drank coffee. She had a boyfriend when she first arrived and it had seemed pretty safe together. At first, they and their group of friends would find places to hide at night. Golden Gate Park or the beach were common places for homeless kids that roamed the streets of the Haight District, pan handling or getting high in the day time. Gradually, all their other friends moved on. They either went back to classes at Humbolt or called their parents for money and went home when they got tired of being on the street.

Those that stayed had few opportunities to get off the street once they were out there. You can't really go for a job interview dressed in the filthy clothes you've been wearing on the street for days. Even if you get a shower and a change of clothes at a shelter, there is still the problem of how to keep up appearances once you get a job.

Everybody has their own way of getting by. Some would just rough it and get meals at the various soup kitchens around the city, getting in line for a room at a shelter, getting in when they could. Others, like some of Vince and Eli's friends, who were more streetwise, would work the system until they could fake their way into subsidized housing. This system was one of San Francisco's failed efforts at providing housing for the homeless. There were family housing units for those with children, but you could wait years to get into an apartment. For single people, you had to have a job and a certain amount of money to get into low income housing. It was a scam, really. No one who had an income low enough to qualify for subsidized housing ever had enough money for the three months deposit required to get in. Everybody worked the system somehow. Those with a little money, or a pension would sometimes pool their money with one person signing the lease and the other becoming a midnight roommate. Others might borrow money from relatives or they actually made more than they should have and doctored the application to qualify.

The young street people have a chance. Girls sometimes find relative safety with a boyfriend. It may not get them off the street, but at least they are protected from attacks, if they are with a man. Amy and her boyfriend were one of these young couples, standing in lines at soup kitchens, panhandling for a few dollars a day, and probably stealing when they couldn't persuade enough tourists to contribute to their welfare.

I was no fool, I knew that drugs were part of this lifestyle. But there are worse dangers lurking in the underbelly of the city. Street people occasionally get offered day jobs. It could be hanging pamphlets or posters around town, or working a one day shift for a small shipping company. Once in a while, they even get extras work on a local for a film. Amy and her friend got the rare offer to actually have parts in an independent film. It was supposed to be a sex film, but they figured it would be alright since they would be together.

It wasn't a sex film. There was sex in the beginning, but the director kept pushing them to go farther and farther into acts that would shock the audience. They both became reluctant and not a little scared at the direction things were going. When they protested that they didn't want to go any farther, they were held down and drugged. Amy woke up the next morning lying on the bathroom floor in clothes that were soaking wet. She had passed out and was probably left for dead. She remembered both her and the boyfriend being held down and beaten and she remembered being held underwater in the bathtub. Everything else was a blur, coming in short flashes; what she was sure of was her life was in danger. All signs of the film crew were gone when she woke up alone the next morning. The boyfriend was never seen again. She made some inquiries among the few people she trusted, but no one had seen him. She was afraid to ask further, because the people who made the film were still around. She'd seen one or two of the crew members on the street since and had pretended she didn't recognize them. She was pretty sure they thought she didn't remember anything. Or at least she hoped so.

Vince had taken her in shortly after that and had been trying to persuade her to go back to Eureka where these guys wouldn't find her. She was reluctant and he didn't try to push too hard for fear she'd just turn around and come back. The street can suck you in like that. When the fall semester at Humbolt was ready to start, he finally convinced her to go back and reenroll. Vince told me about the trip back to Eureka; he seemed pleased.

"It was time," he said.

I never saw her again after that night. Vince said not to worry, it was best if no one from this part of her life ever contacted her again. This was her second chance, it was all up to her now.

29 CHANCE MEETING

San Francisco is famous for its unusual characters. Some are amusing, but in real life these characters are usually wounded souls. Life is precious; the strange behaviors or physical suffering we see from a distance mask much deeper psychological suffering that happens when circumstances kill hope.

There was a well turned out trans woman who used to take the same bus or trolley I so often used. One day when we both got off at the same stop and were walking in the same direction, I mentioned that I often saw her on the same route as myself. I complimented her on how nice she always looked. I was on my way home and I asked, if she lived in the same neighborhood.

She must have somehow felt comfortable talking to me, because she answered without hesitation. I was used to the fact that anything goes in San Francisco, but her reply floored me.

"Well, sometimes I stay in the alley behind the shopping mall. Other times, I have a place that I can stay in the financial district after everything closes down."

You would have never guessed she was homeless. She was smart though. Dressing well meant she wasn't attracting attention to herself. She wouldn't be targeted by police or security officers as a transient. If she was careful, she could find an out of the way corner to sleep while things were closed down and she wouldn't have to worry about being harassed by other street people, or the authorities.

I asked her if she couldn't find a way to get an apartment, but she said she couldn't work. I didn't ask any more questions about that; it was going to be a story that was hard to hear and I couldn't do anything about.

She didn't dwell on that. She said she was dressed up tonight because she had a date and she was so excited. She was looking for love, but probably also someone to take care of her. I didn't judge her for that; she needed someone. There are a lot of people in San Francisco who get along by dating. Sometimes it's the only time they get a meal that isn't from a soup kitchen.

I wished her a good evening and said I hoped she had a good time. Then we parted ways. God only knows what she had to do on those dates. I hoped she would find someone and get off the street. A few weeks later, I noticed her hiding her face against the wall at a building not far from where I lived. I was on a bus, but I could see her clearly enough to tell she was crying.

I thought, "There but for the grace of God, go I."

Like the fallen society type I had seen on another day, none of us know what is coming next and any one of us could be taking the place of one of those people we walk past every day and ignore.

30 THE SAN FRANCISCO HIKER

It's not all sadness, though there are the other types who are just eccentric and harmless. I called my favorite the Naked Hiker. The first time I saw him I was on a bus on one of those connecting streets that's busy, but not a main thoroughfare. It was a foggy, slightly chilly morning and the windows were starting to steam up as it got more crowded. But suddenly everyone on the bus was looking to the left. I was standing up, but I had to lean in to see over all the other passengers who were gawking. It takes a lot to make San Franciscans take a second look. But just when you think you've seen everything; there it is, a sight you've never seen before.

There was a man, about six feet two; shaved head, as was the fashion at the time; wearing only hiking boots and socks. He was strutting along at a good pace and obviously enjoying the walk, as well as the attention!

He was actually a fixture in San Francisco for a while. I worked down by the wharf and I actually saw him from the window of the gallery a couple of times, walking down by the little park along the shoreline. He must have really enjoyed those walks. When I first saw him he was probably in his thirties, quite fit and trim. I didn't expect he would be around for very long, but I actually saw him several years later. He was wearing the same scanty outfit, and he'd gained a few pounds, but it was him, for sure.

I often wondered how many times he got picked up by the San Francisco police. SFPD must have gotten used to him after a while. They must have had a phone number of someone to call to come bring clothes. Compared to their other guests, he must have been just a minor inconvenience.

31 THE BOND THIEF

Most people don't realize that everything east of The Palace Hotel on Market Street stands on a land fill. After the Gold Rush, all the ships on the docks were abandoned and left to rot. The area around China Town, which was known as the Barbary Coast, fell farther into Dickensian wretchedness and became the Red Light District.

Eventually, the city filled that area in and now it's home to the lonely high rises offices and hotels of the financial district and a small shopping mall leading to Justin Herman Plaza. A few of the older brick buildings on the north side bordering China Town still exist, and one particular bar in that area is noted for a window where you can look down and see the remains of a ship buried beneath it. Market street ends just across the street from the Ferry Plaza, making that a central terminus for all the major transportation lines. You can go from ferry boats, to cable car, bus, high speed rail, underground metro, or walk the shoreline all the way to Giants Stadium from there. Everybody ends up there at one time or another whether they are residents, commuters, or tourists. You see all kinds of people down there.

After working in the financial district, my eye for people became more acute. As I walked along Market Street in that area, I would watch the people and imagine who they were and where they were going. I could recognize the financial workers, they were the ones in the suits. It was the only place in San Francisco where suits were fairly common. I could guess who were the top dogs and who were the young hungry brokers by the cut of their suits. The people in colorful shirts and shorts were tourists. Locals never wore shorts. It just wasn't done. At that time, locals wore mainly jeans and hoodies in dark colors. It made for a dark view on the buses in the local neighborhoods.

One day, as I was walking toward Market Street on the west side of Third, when I noticed a young man coming out of the Hearst Building. I don't know why he caught my eye, maybe it was just the silhouette created by the ill fitting suit and the hair, a little too long for a business man. As I turned the corner and continued north up Market Street the young man crossed the street and came up beside me.

"Mind if I walk with you for a bit?"

This sounded suspiciously like a come on, yet strangely out of place. I was still young enough to attract male attention at times, but not from any one in their twenties. He did have a plan, though. He fell in step with me and began asking me about something banal, like the weather. Before he finished his sentence, three older men in black suits came at us from different directions. They moved in rapidly in a well orchestrated move that stopped my companion dead in his tracks and left me continuing up Market Street without even breaking stride. Whatever this guy was doing in the Hearst Building, it wasn't good and I was expecting to be arrested right along with him as an accomplice.

It all happened so fast. One moment they were closing in and the next they had they had a hold on my strange new acquaintance. I stopped dead a few paces on and looked back, surprised to see the arrest taking place without the slightest disturbance of foot traffic. He was being cuffed by one of them while another was taking his brief case.

The third one said, "We've got you this time."

To my relief, they weren't even looking at me. I was curious about this, but not enough to hang around. I turned and walked up Market Street, relieved and astonished at having made a cameo appearance in a scene that could have been right out of a movie. But it was real, it was done so quietly. It was San Francisco, anything can happen. But I'll always wonder what it was this time.

32 ABE

It was just over two hours, less than one hundred and fifty miles from San Francisco to Grass Valley. I had been in San Francisco for nearly six months, but I hadn't been to visit Abe. I had been caught up with surviving. Learning to live in an apartment building where I was being threatened by my neighbors, living on just enough to get by, and going from job to job. When I lost theater, I lost my way. I had no direction, no goals, no point to my life.

Abe had just had his second by-pass surgery at eighty-three years old. Soon there would be no more chances. The heart surgery had been successful, but he had now had short term memory loss. A brilliant mind was fading. I didn't know what to expect, but I wanted to see him, I needed to see him while he was doing well and his memory loss was confined to small things.

Abe and his wife Leti had become my surrogate grandparents when I moved to California at age seventeen. I was alienated from my own family and never experienced a family relationship that was supportive and nonjudgmental. I could go to Abe and Leti about anything. They would listen, they would encourage, and they would give advice about how to achieve my own goals, not the goals they had for me.

Abe was the son of Russian Jewish immigrants and Leti was a devote Catholic who had immigrated to the US from Puerto Rico as a college student. They both believed in the promise of America, having grown up in a time when dreams were still possibilities. They admired and respected each other as people. The supported each other in their life goals and did not let religious differences allow them to deny their human bonds.

They were members and supporters of the Baha'i faith. The Baha'i faith is one of the most modern but lesser known western religions. They see themselves as the obvious modern descendant of the three main religions, which all originated in the middle east. So, their beliefs encompassed, Judaism, Christianity, and Islam, and the a later prophet known as the **Bahá'u'lláh**. To put it in the simplest terms, it's function was to bring all the major western religions together and bring them into the modern world.

It worked for them. Neither of them had to deny their familial religion, yet they could embrace the more modern goals of the Baha'i faith. As educators, they praised the Baha'i custom of educating women. The custom was based on simple practical logic. If a family could afford to educate only one of their children, they would educate the oldest girl; because as a sister and a mother she would have the responsibility of educating the children. So, that education would not be lost on one person whose central goal was their personal career.

The other thing they strongly supported about the Baha'i Faith was that it supported the United Nations. The Baha'i faith teaches that we should be good citizens, as well as good family members. They are believers in peace and, as such, feel a responsibility to world peace. They believe that only by all nations coming together can world peace be maintained.

There are some serious political issues with this faith and I am by no means proselytizing. I describe the faith here in the simplest terms to demonstrate the bond between two important mentors in my life. They were two people with different backgrounds and temperaments. Yet they came together through loving kindness and a similar world view. They were not over zealous about their religion, but saw it as a very practical religious world view and one most suitable to their personal beliefs. I never became a Baha'i, but exposure this religious belief which had such a strong focus on world peace, lead me to be more accepting of all forms of religion based in loving kindness and unity.

***

Abe was a person who took action. He had been a pharmacist for twenty years before he became a teacher. Once he decided to make the change, he devoted himself to it wholeheartedly. He and Leti met while teaching in Los

Angeles. Abe already had in mind the move to Grass Valley. He loved teaching, but wanted a more peaceful life, which he felt he could find in Northern California.

They had both been married before and were not in a rush to marry again. Leti only agreed to marry Abe when he finalized his arrangements to move north and asked her to go with him. It was a good match. They both had long teaching careers in the local school district. They had the house and garden they always wanted; Abe even created a Japanese garden. When they were ready to retire, Abe bought a smaller property and built a self sufficient house, which was mostly off the grid. Then the gardening began again and soon there was a pond big enough for the grandchildren to swim in and gardens with crushed granite walks that allowed Leti to continue enjoying them even after her arthritis forced her to walk with a cane. There was even a greenhouse with solar panels that adjusted the light and temperature automatically.

Abe was a person who was knowledgeable on many subjects . He had been an art major in his undergraduate days and still had some of his art work from the early days. The work in pharmacy needed a background in science, yet when he became a teacher, it was social studies that became his passion. He felt it was so important that students have an understanding of the world, if we were going to have informed citizens tomorrow.

Leti had been a Spanish teacher in L.A. but changed to special education when they moved north. She took her first class of learning impaired students from a class of lazy students who were used to having no expectations, to students who never used their learning challenges as an excuse. All graduated and were gainfully employed. Leti was a fantastic teacher and homemaker. I could talk to her about my fiber art projects and she understood. It wasn't domesticity, it was creativity.

They were my home away from home. They made me feel valued as a person in a way that no other people did. They were the family I never had. Time, distance and life's challenges limited the amount of time I could spend with them, but every moment was precious.

As they aged and Leti's arthritis became worse, she was in a lot of pain. On these later visits, I would sit on the veranda and keep her company while Abe was out working around the property. Abe was not a person to sit still for long, he always had some new project going.

Eventually, Leti had trouble getting around. She could no longer cook or do the house work, making it hard on Abe. He loved her, but he was not a caregiver. On my last visit with Leti she talked about how difficult it was to be in pain all the time. She never complained. But on this day, she told me she was ready for God to take her. She did not want to suffer any more. That was the last time I saw her. It was difficult for me to hear. I did not want to lose Leti, but also, I did not want her to suffer. I wasn't sure what was the right thing to say. Finally, I said, "I think it's ok to let go." No one else ever knew of this conversation. I'm still not sure it was the right thing to say, but it seemed right at the time. I felt she was holding on for Abe and I didn't want her to feel guilty about leaving him. She passed away later that year.

Abe carried on alone for a while, but within a year, he had remarried. Some people just cannot live alone after a long marriage.

His new wife was completely different from Leti. I could see she was not a person I could be close to. But she took care of Abe, not that he wasn't able to do some things for himself. Since the operation though, the memory loss prevented him from doing things that had been routine before. The short term memory loss prevented him from doing math or any tasks that required holding numbers or words in his mind to complete a structured task. He was no long able to balance a check book, which left his second wife in charge of the financial affairs.

That day, I got a chance to ask him about his early life in New York City. He listened to my plans for the future and gave what advise he could. Things were different now. I had a teaching credential, but unlike when Abe changed his career in mid-life, they weren't looking for older teachers now. It was one more dream that lead me down an unexpected path. I never got to teach in an American public school, instead I took the only teaching job I could find; teaching English in Asia. It wasn't my dream, but it did allow me to travel places and experience things I never would have otherwise. Often times, it's the tradeoff that makes the best experiences in life.

It was a good visit. I left before the light started failing. I was in a rented car and I didn't want to be driving back over the Bay Bridge into San Francisco in the dark. Besides, I could see the wife was waiting for me to leave before she started dinner. I wasn't going to be invited.

I gave Abe a last hug and headed out down the dirt road toward the main road into town. It was the end of an era. Betty had died while I was in college in Oregon, Ken and Michael were both gone. Now Abe was my last connection to my old life. Their were no more mentors. I knew now that I was totally alone.

33 OCEAN BEACH MYSTERY HOUSE

San Francisco has one of the best transportation systems in the United States. It includes buses, trolleys, cable cars, a subway system, and rapid transit. But it is possible to walk anywhere in the city. On a good day, I could walk all the way from downtown, where I lived, through Golden Gate Park and out to the beach at the Outer Richmond area.

When I first moved there, the Cliff house was still a cozy restaurant with an ocean view on two sides, known to locals for fresh popovers available at breakfast. The Cliff House website notes four different renovations of the building, but fails to mention the remodeling that took place between 2003 and 2004. This final renovation eliminated any hint of establishment's historic appearance. They still have popovers, but the menu is pricier and in my opinion not as good quality as it was in the ten years or so prior to this last remodeling. One more affordable restaurant with great breakfasts bites the dust in San Francisco.

However, it is still well worth the trip out to this far west end of the Golden Gate Recreation Area. You can still explore the Sutro Bath ruins, which was once a large complex of public baths and swimming pools that operated until 1964, when it closed due to high operating costs. The building was destroyed but the remains are still there and it's fun to explore the grounds and the haunting remains. The pump house was located in a cave and you can still go through there to a hidden section of the beach at low tide.

Above the Cliff House and the ruins of the Sutro Baths there is a pleasant park where the old Sutro estate used to overlook the highway. It's a relaxing place for a picnic and seldom crowded, as most people don't notice it as the drive down Point Lobos Avenue approaching Ocean Beach. I used to take the bus out there and get off at the last stop before the beach. Sutro

Heights Park was just across the highway.

The mystery was, what was that abandoned house just to the south of the park? I discovered this one day when I was looking for a way to get up to the lookout from the south side with a picnic lunch I'd purchased at the market nearby. Heading north on the first street over from the highway, the ridge rises straight up and there's no more street. But there was a wooden walkway that goes up the cliff and out to the street just behind the park. At the turn in the trail, there was a chain link fence overgrown with ivy. I could peak through and see a backyard with a large oak tree and the ruins of a private garden. The house in front faced the street near where the downtown bus stop was. It, too was fenced off and was obviously in ruins. It wasn't a mansion, but you could see by the front portico and large windows that it had once been an elegant house. There were no markers to indicate if it was owned by the park or was private property, just the usual "Keep Out" warnings. I wish I had been adventurous enough to sneak in there. It was not a place you would notice easily. There was a lot of overgrown vegetation in the front as well. In fact, I had walked past it on several occasions and thought it was part of the grounds of a newer house next door. It didn't seem to be vandalized. There was no visible graffiti on the outside, possibly because this was an upscale neighborhood that wasn't inviting to vagrants. It's probably a good thing I didn't go in there, but I have it in my imagination and it's tucked away for a story sometime in the future.

There are a lot of hidden gems in San Francisco. I'd love to go back and revisit them someday to write a little secret tour book for the curious traveler. It could happen!

34 SCHERENSCHNITTE

But what about Portland? In a way, Portland was a microcosm of what I would experience in San Francisco. It was a small city, but still diverse, and had all the perils and adventures awaiting that might be found in larger cities. They were both among the most walkable cities in America. The light rail system in Portland had opened just before I left.

Until then, buses were the only public transportation. So, I often found myself walking. You might as well have walked to anything less than two miles away. The buses ran on twenty to thirty minute intervals and if one didn't come at the scheduled time, it probably wasn't coming. I didn't mind. I ended up living just a few blocks from friends in the Northwest District. Like any city, a matter of a few blocks can change the atmosphere of the neighborhood. Their house was in an older district that was gradually becoming gentrified, while I lived in a rooming house, equally old, but obviously designed for a more working class neighborhood. Still, it was safe and pleasant to walk around the neighborhood.

I loved exploring the area with all the old Victorian houses. Each one had it's own character. You might have a spruced up house newly purchased, by a young yuppie couple right next to a slightly shabby one where an older couple lived, who might be the second or third generation to have grown up in that house. Some of the houses had been preserved by dividing them into two or three apartments with separate entrances. Each owner had a different way of making the dwelling they loved work for them. Everyone loved being part of the neighborhood.

One snowy evening just before Christmas, I was walking around enjoying all the decorations, when I noticed a light in a basement window. I tried not to peak into these windows as I walked by. I had lived in a basement in college and know how ground level windows can reduce privacy. But this one was decorated! I approached a little closer to see what was there. It wasn't a tree, it was all white. Was it a snow scene? It was blocked off with a white background, giving the appearance of a miniature stage. As I got closer, I could see it was a Christmas scene. There was a paper fireplace with an paper man in a rocking chair, a woman in an old fashioned frock was bringing a tray of tea and cookies to the man. There was a fully decorated Christmas tree in the corner, a rug on the floor and even a dog by the fire.

Everything was in miniature and quite three dimensional. There was a lacy texture to the whole scene as if it had been built from snowflakes. It was the first time I had ever seen Scherenschnitte, the intricate German art of paper cutting. What a holiday treat!

I would soon encounter more Scherenschnitte in a more bold form. The following year, a friend of mine asked me to make his costume for the annual Halloween Ball. It's now called the Erotic Halloween Ball, but I don't remember the emphasis being on eroticism at that time. There were some sexy costumes, but not as the main focus. It was the biggest costume ball in Portland and this was like the Mardi Gras. You could tell, some people had been working on their costumes for a year. Sexy costumes can't compare. It doesn't take much to put together a glittery G-string and some pasties, but to create a costume that is imaginatively conceived and expertly executed is a serious task. This costume ball was seriously competitive!

They had hired a warehouse for the event and they needed every inch of it. David was dressed in a sort of generic genie costume with flowing shirt, wide draped pants, a knee length brocade vest, soft boots, and a turban I had taught him how to wrap. Nothing fancy, but nice for a small budget costume, and one I thought he could embellish each year to make it gradually become much grander. I was an Egyptian queen complete with gold lame snake headdress. David was helping out at the AIDS awareness booth. When I arrived he took his break so we could both mingle. After all, if you weren't there for the costume prize, you definitely wanted to see who might be the winners. There were a lot of amazing costumes, but there were two that stood out for me. Of course, both won prizes. The first was a truck costume. Imagine Mater from the movie Cars, only this was long before that movie came out. He had built a truck out of lightweight material, complete with working headlights. He could just fit into the cab with the whole costume supported by suspender-like shoulder straps. It made quite a picture as he flashed those headlights around the dance floor. He got second place. The winner was yet to appear.

In the meantime, David introduced me to an old friend he'd run into and hardly recognized.

"Hello, David."

"Roger?"

"Yes, I haven't dressed up in a long time, but every once in a while, I have to trot out the old finery, just to show I can still do it."

This was my first up close look at a drag queen in full regalia. I saw a lot more of this in San Francisco, but to be honest, this was the most impressive drag outfit, I've ever seen. She was decked out in an Elizabethan costume with the high wig, big puffed sleeves, and cartwheel hoop skirt. She had the make up right and the sequined eyelashes, which would have been ridiculous on an average sized woman, were the perfect finish to the face of this six foot two drag queen. They had just the right flash for the club lights. We hit it off right away. S/he was no slouch with the stitching and I didn't hesitate to pick her brain about how she made some of the more challenging parts of the costume work.

Then all records were broken. The rolling doors had to be opened to allow for the entrance of the next couple. The Wicked Witch of the West marched in holding the hand of Glenda the Good Witch! The Wicked Witch was all green skin and black robes, pointy hat and pointy shoes. Glenda was Hollywood perfection! The sea of people parted for them. The tall hat, the five foot wide hooped skirt, and the balloon sleeves were all made of paper lace! She held her hand out regally for the companion, who's job it was to carefully clear the way.

The lower sleeves were made of tubes covered in cut paper lace, so she could not but hold her arms out in a ballerina like pose above the flowing skirt. She was covered in Scherenschnitte, head to toe, It was the Christmas window guy, it had to be!

35 HOTEL EL RANCHO

It was my last road trip. I was going to take the southwest route across Arizona and New Mexico continuing east all the way to Nashville. I had already driven the northern and the central routes, so this would tick the last cross country United States interstate drive off my list. I-40 follows most of old Route 66, which was called the Mother Road because it was the first interstate that went all the way from the east coast to the west coast. It's still the easiest drive. There are no dangerous mountain passes or interchanges to negotiate Just sit back and drive. The only disadvantage is that it is mostly a due east west route. I was traveling from the San Francisco Bay Area, so I was able to pick up I-40 in Fresno to avoid driving all the way south to Los Angeles.

I had been staying with my friends Tom and Elaine in Lafayette and I wanted to get an early start. It was a thousand miles to Gallup, New Mexico. So, I planned on stopping somewhere in Arizona the first night. I made good time and arrived in Bakersfield, where I picked up I-40, which I would follow the rest of the way into Tennessee. But I was making good time and I passed Bakersfield in less than four hours. Barstow was farther east and closer to the Arizona border, but it was a lot smaller than I expected. I kept on straight into Arizona. I wasn't prepared for how desolate the next leg of the trip was going to be. I finally found a small motel off a dirt road somewhere outside of Kingman, when I realized there might not be any more stops until Flagstaff, which would be much too far.

The next morning I was feeling good and only stopped for gas and meals. It was still light when I got to Flagstaff, so I decided to keep going until I got tired. As I passed Flagstaff and got closer to the New Mexico border, the landscape changed. There were buttes and strange landforms in every direction. I was in a badlands area, possibly part of the Painted Desert. I've since tried to identify that part of the trip and it's not clear on any map what the area is called. But it was eerie. If it had been broad daylight, it would have seemed desolate and maybe a little boring. But the sun was going down and as the low light hit the west facing sides of the cliffs they turned all shades of color from orange to purple. I don't know what the desert looks like around Santa Fe, but I was imagining Georgia O'Keefe with her easel in the desert, watching a sunset like this.

It was dark by the time I got to Gallup and unlike the exits along most of California's I-5, motels and restaurants did not hug the roads around every exit. But just past the main part of Gallup, I saw a motel. It was all light up in neon like something out of a 1950s movie. I pulled off to get a better look. It was a long low-slung ranch style building with a rail fence around the parking lot. The big neon sign would have read Hotel El Rancho, if all the letters had been lit. It had a large portico entrance and was two stories with two single story wings one either side. You could see it was a nice building in a distinct southwest period style. It had actually been built in the 1930s. Along the porch roofline, it read "Charm of yesterday and the convenience of tomorrow." That slogan must have been there from the day they opened.

I needed to stop for the night and I couldn't miss this.

Inside, The big central lobby was decorated with heavy ranch style couches and arm chairs covered in rough textured upholstery striped in colors reminiscent of the colors against the rocky cliffs I'd seen at sunset earlier that evening. There were a few taxidermied remains of local wildlife on the walls along with a set of horns from what could only have been a Texas Longhorn Steer above the stairs. But mainly the walls were decorated with photos of movie stars, directors, crew members and location shots from all the different movie crews members who'd stayed here while shooting western movies. Display cases contained handmade jewelry from well known Native American artists and there was a small, well appointed shop where you could purchase some of the finest silver work in the south west. I'd seen a lot of American and Mexican made jewelry in shops all around the American west. Most of it was mass produced and quality varied from the typical jewelry store products to signed pieces. I'm no expert on this craft, but it was easy to see these were not ordinary pieces. Every piece was beautifully worked, no rough edges like you often see on work at street fairs, yet the pieces had weight and the details had depth you don't see in mass produced jewelry. There was no little turn cart with jewelry on cards. Each piece was displayed under glass and lit to enhance the beauty of the handwork. There was nothing in those glass cases that I could afford; they were all too special.

My room was a small little cubby in the back with a tiny bathroom, a sink by the door and an old fashioned radiator next to the window. The bed was comfortable and there was a serviceable desk in one corner. It was nothing special, but then I could afford it. Each room was named after a movie actor. Beginning with early talkies right up to the late sixties when westerns finally died out as an American film style. But that's one of the nice things about this hotel, they are set up to accommodate road weary travelers like me right alongside of people who need a bit more pampering in the upper rooms.

This had been a popular hotel for film crews from the very earliest days of Hollywood. It had all the scenic backdrops that might be needed nearby. The entire crew could be accommodated here, driven out to shooting locations each day, and be fed in the large ranch style dining hall in the basement. As I walked the gallery of portraits, I wondered what stories the old hotel staff shared from back in the early days when actors like Errol Flynn, John Wayne, or Gene Autry stayed there. The ladies were there too; Mae West, Jean Harlow, and even Jane Fonda had stayed here.

You could see why this hotel attracted visitors to the southwest. It was close enough to the Grand Canyon and several other national parks to enjoy the beauty of this wide open piece of American history, yet offered all the comforts lacking in so many roadside hotels. To be honest, this is one of the last areas left in the United States where there isn't a Holiday Inn or Best Western at almost every exit. Exits are few and far between. Gallup is a town of only about 20, 000 people and it's 140 miles to Albuquerque from there, with nothing much in between.

There's a nice bar on the ground floor and a big dining room in the basement. The dining room is interesting because it serves good food, it's reasonably priced, and it is still designed to serve everyone in one large space. It's not over decorated, just comfortable but practical. This story isn't meant to recommend tourist spots. Most of the places I've stopped and the things I've done on my road trips, I don't recommend readers to try. That's why they are stories. But I would recommend Hotel El Rancho. If you want to stay somewhere comfortable with a bit of history, this hotel is a great jumping off place for anyone planning to spend time in the southwest or just passing through.

The next morning when I went out to the parking lot, I had a flat tire. I had hit the curb coming in the night before. It had been a new moon that night; there were no streetlights; and I was dead tired, I had driven ten hours straight and should have stopped in Flagstaff. So, I had made a mistake. The tire didn't go flat right away. I found out later, I had bent the rim. So, the tire had been leaking all night and it was totally flat.

I went back in and asked the desk clerk if she knew of a reliable repair shop. I would need to change the tire and drive into Gallup. But I was worried about getting over charged because of the out of state license plates on a rented car.

"I know you aren't supposed to give recommendations, but I am sure this isn't the first time a visitor has needed an auto shop while staying here. Any shop you can recommend, even if it's just on a business card from a previous lodger would be better than choosing a place at random from the yellow pages."

The yellow pages, do they even have that anymore? They had cell phones, but this area was still a dead zone.

As she was searching the phone lists they had, I couldn't help but notice how beautiful she was. She had perfectly balanced features, sleek black hair hanging below her waist, and that warm glowing skin tone that you only see in Native American people. This is just a personal reaction. Don't get all scientific on me. I don't know if it's the cheekbones, the jawline, or the eyes. But this woman would have stood out in a crowd anywhere. Out from behind that counter, dressed up and walking down a city street, she would have stopped traffic. But you could tell she wasn't that type. She had an inward calm, she wouldn't have been showing off.

She had just found a number for me and I was about to call and get directions, when a man about her age came up to the counter.

"It's ok," he said to her and turned to me. "You don't have to call. I know where to go. I'll change your tire for you and go with you to the shop. My buddies work there. I'll make sure they treat you right."

I was surprised. Normally, I would have been hesitant about a stranger offering to help and then taking me some place I didn't know. But the desk clerk seemed to know him and didn't object.

It wasn't a long drive, but long enough for him to tell me his story. We started out talking about the hotel and all the film people that had stayed there. Then he was telling me about how the jewelry store got started. In the Southwest, there are silver mines and the Native American people in this area are famous for their silver work, as well as weaving, and pottery.

Eventually, the expeditors for the film crews got to know the best silversmiths and started commissioning them to make special pieces for films. That's how the shop ended up with all the well known silversmiths work. Of course, this is a niche market and the names are only known by collectors, but it is a market with customers who have the money for custom made pieces.

William started talking about different movies that have silver from people he knew and modestly said he had work in one film. You can see his silver work in a well known film from classic American literature. The silver and turquoise wrist bands can be seen in the funeral scene at the end of the movie. He was just getting started as a silversmith and this was a sale that could bring a lot more work his way.

There was a lot more to that story, but I won't tell it here. It's enough to say he was a kind man and seem happy to be with his beautiful wife. I never mentioned her physical beauty, just her beautiful spirit.

He waited with me and I gave him a lift back to the hotel. I paid him for his trouble and he didn't turn down the money. But he didn't seem like he expected it. Maybe he just needed to tell his story.

People like to tell their stories to strangers. There's less judgment and maybe it helps them let go of whatever it is that's making them hold onto the story. I actually got my dental hygienists divorce story one afternoon while she cleaned my teeth. I had to listen; there were instruments in my mouth.

Vanity Card

Did you know that Chuck Lorre put a vanity card at the end of each episode of *The Big Bang Theory*?

Vanity cards have a long history. Today the term is a synonym for a trademark or logo used in the motion picture, television, and more recently in the gaming industry. Chuck Lorre invented a unique form of vanity card in which he inserts short essays or editorials at the end of each production. It's not possible to read them as the credits roll, but with today's technology a curious person can stop motion to read them. They are usually quite funny.

It's as if he has planted little Easter eggs in every production. You know Easter eggs don't' you? Those are the little hidden jokes, put accidentally on purpose in many of the Disney animations by the animators.

I enjoy vanity cards. So, I see no reason why I can't do it, too. It's fun and I can check to see if you've read, or listened, as the case may be, to the whole story.

You may be saying to yourself, "Vanity, indeed! Who does she think she is?

I'm a person who's always trying out new things. I especially like to try out new words or expressions. If you are wondering why I vainly wrote about myself; me, a nobody, in my first book. Maybe this will help.

When I was in the first grade, I told my older brother that when I got older I was going to have a diarrhea. He laughed. Offended, I demanded to know why he was laughing. Between laughs and trying to catch his breathe, he said,

"Go tell Mom what you said."

When I repeated my declaration to Mom, she handed me a page from the paper she was reading and said,

"You better take this you might have one now."

That was how I found out there were two very similar words.

Now, you are probably saying to yourself,

"But your first statement was true. This effort is a bunch of diarrhea!"

I say to you, " If you've gotten this far, you must be wrong."

You will just have to bear with me.

I did keep diaries during my early travel days and some of these stories came from them. But as I wrote, I found a lot of short episodes that I never thought I would write about came tumbling back to me. So, what's the point? I've always kept diaries. What is the use? Well, as Mae West once said, " I think everybody should keep a diary. You never, know it might mean something to someone someday." I hope these stories have meant something to you.

Appendix

Prologue
Hurricane Donna (September 11, 1960)
https://en.wikipedia.org/wiki/Hurricane_Donna
Giant City Park
https://www.dnr.illinois.gov/Parks/Pages/GiantCity.aspx
St. Louis Zoo https://www.stlzoo.org/visit/local-visit?gclid=Cj0KCQjwyvXPBRD-ARIsAIeQeoEoPaUu9V53ZUltZIAyc5um5I0bRfaCCjJrs0gQww7nZB9VCiCqPTIaAup2EALw_wcB
St. Louis Art Museum http://www.slam.org/
Lizzie Borden http://famous-trials.com/lizzieborden

Honolulu
Honolulu Zoo http://honoluluzoo.org/
The Punch Bowl https://www.youtube.com/watch?v=0FaRgOzSBwg
Kilauea Volcano https://www.youtube.com/watch?v=888nbjvkNts

L.A.
1938 Dodge Touring Car http://www.classiccarcatalogue.com/DODGE%201938.html *Boulevard Nights* http://www.imdb.com/title/tt0078898/ How fast can you travel https://www.mnn.com/green-tech/transportation/stories/how-fast-could-you-travel-across-the-us-in-the-1800s

The Definition of Success
Renaissance Pleasure Faire
  http://framework.latimes.com/2014/04/25/renaissance-pleasure-faire-at-paramount-ranch/#/0
Card weaving or tablet weaving
https://en.wikipedia.org/wiki/Tablet_weaving
Kaffe Fassett http://https://en.wikipedia.org/wiki/Kaffe_Fassett

An Open Door
Dusky Canada Goose
http://creagrus.home.montereybay.com/MTYbirdsCACG.html

Mary Ellen
It's OK If You Sit On My Quilt
https://en.wikipedia.org/wiki/Mary_Ellen_Hopkins

Columbia Gorge
Mount Hood National Forest https://www.fs.usda.gov/mthood
Grapevine Hill http://forums.vintage-mustang.com/vintage-mustang-forum/386827-o-t-follow-up-hot-rod-lincoln-where-grapevine-hill.htmlMap of the San Francisco Bay
bike ride http://palaceoffinearts.org/

The East Coast
Dam dolls http://mentalfloss.com/article/88225/12-hair-raising-facts-about-troll-dolls
Jelly's Last Jam https://en.wikipedia.org/wiki/Jell%27s_Last_Jam
Ken
American Kennel Club http://www.akc.org/dog-breeds/samoyed/
Alaskan Malamute https://g.co/kgs/mtTfmG

Revenge
The Costume Collection https://www.tdf.org/nyc/30/TDF-Costume-Collection

The Southwest Route
Celtic dance https://g.co/kgs/NNWFZN
River Dance **https://g.co/kgs/pNEET**Chapter 27 - Michael
Yoshi's https://www.yoshis.com/
Beach Chalet https://www.beachchalet.com/

Green Card
Glide https://www.glide.org/
Tenderloin http://www.sfgate.com/neighborhoods/sf/tenderloin/
The Mark https://en.wikipedia.org/wiki/Mark_Hopkins_Hotel

Ex-cons
The Castro Neighborhood
https://en.wikipedia.org/wiki/Castro_District,_San_Francisco

The Bond Thief
Justin Herman Plaza https://www.nbcbayarea.com/news/local/SF-Leaders-Vote-Unanimously-to-Rename-Justin-Herman-Plaza-445886603.html
Buried ships in San Francisco https://news.nationalgeographic.com/2017/05/map-ships-buried-san-francisco/
Hearst Building (The Hearst website has been hacked. At this time, I am offering an image gallery.) https://www.bluffton.edu/homepages/facstaff/sullivanm/jmhearst/jmhearst.html

Abe
Grass Valley https://en.wikipedia.org/wiki/Grass_Valley,_California

Ocean Beach Mystery House
Cliff House_
http://cliffhouse1.reachlocal.net/ch_accessible/ac_history/today.html

Scherenschnitte
Scherenschnitte https://en.wikipedia.org/wiki/Scherenschnitte

Hotel El Rancho
Route 66 https://en.wikipedia.org/wiki/U.S._Route_66
Painted Desert https://en.wikipedia.org/wiki/Painted_Desert_(Arizona)

ABOUT THE AUTHOR

This is a first novel for Joy Harmon. She is a wanderer who has driven solo across the United States three times, lived in a half dozen different states, and worked in a variety of occupations. Along the way, she has been a keen observer of life. This book represents some of her observations.

She considers life a journey where the people and personalities she's met along the way are part of the rich spice of life.

Future project plans include a fictional history of San Francisco and another novel based on her great grandmother's Native American background and family legends..

Made in the USA
Middletown, DE
15 October 2021